SEEKING THE
HEART *of*
CHRIST

SEEKING THE
HEART *of*
CHRIST

Christian Reflections on the Interior Life

SAINT CLAUDE
LA COLOMBIÈRE

Compiled and translated by
BRANDON P. OTTO

TAN Books
Gastonia, North Carolina

English translation copyright © 2025 TAN Books

All rights reserved. With the exception of short excerpts used in critical review, no part of this work may be reproduced, transmitted, or stored in any form whatsoever, without the prior written permission of the publisher. Creation, exploitation, and distribution of any unauthorized editions of this work, in any format in existence now or in the future—including but not limited to text, audio, and video—is prohibited without the prior written permission of the publisher.

Compiled and translated by Brandon P. Otto

Cover design by Jordan Avery

Cover image: *Figure of Christ* by Heinrich Hofmann, Public domain, via Wikimedia Commons

ISBN: 978-1-5051-3244-1
Kindle ISBN: 978-1-5051-3641-8
ePUB ISBN: 978-1-5051-3640-1

Published in the United States by
TAN Books
PO Box 269
Gastonia, NC 28053

www.TANBooks.com

Printed in the United States of America

Contents

Translator's Note vii
Note on the Text xi
Notice to the Reader xv
On the Sweetness of Virtue 1
On Desires 11
On Faith 25
On Conscience 39
On Confession 55
On Deferred Repentance 63
On Frequent Communion 71
On the Mass 83
On Irreverence in Churches 97
On Ingratitude 111
On Intemperance 115
On Submission to the Will of God 121

On Impurity 127
On Vainglory 131
On Humility 147
On Adversities 153
On the Mercy of God Towards Sinners 161
On Death 169
On Hell 181
On Paradise 193

Translator's Note

"One must be a saint in order to make saints."¹ Therefore, Claude La Colombière—called to the apostolic life by his Jesuit vocation—had to become a saint, and so he did. La Colombière is best known as the spiritual director of St. Marguerite-Marie Alacoque and a promoter of her devotion to the Sacred Heart. But his true goal was simply to be a saint, and for him, "it is impossible to give a higher idea of sanctity than that of a perfect Jesuit."²

La Colombière was born on February 2, 1641, in Saint-Symphorien-d'Ozon, outside Lyon, to a truly religious family: out of the five children who survived childhood,

---

[1] Claude La Colombière, *Spiritual Journal*, §113, in Claude La Colombière, Écrits spirituels, ed. André Ravier, 2nd ed. (Paris: Desclée de Brouwer/Bellarmin, 1982), 149. The two *Spiritual Retreats* and the *Spiritual Journal* were originally published in one volume, with no section numbering; Ravier's edition numbers their sections sequentially.

[2] Claude La Colombière, *Spiritual Retreat of 1674* §16, in La Colombière, Écrits spirituels, 90.

four became religious, and the one son who married was said to be like "a monk remaining in the world."³ La Colombière entered the Jesuits in 1658 and professed his first vows in 1660; after giving a panegyric to celebrate the canonization of St. Francis de Sales in 1666, he was sent to study theology in Paris, where he was ordained to the priesthood in 1669. After teaching rhetoric for three years, he began his third year of probation in 1674—during which he wrote his first *Spiritual Retreat* and his *Spiritual Journal*—culminating in his solemn vows in 1675. After these vows, he was sent to Paray-le-Monial, where he met St. Marguerite-Marie Alacoque. He declared her revelations of the Sacred Heart to be authentic,⁴ and he became her spiritual director and promoter.

In 1676, La Colombière was sent to London to be the preacher for the Duchess of York, a Catholic. There, he wrote his *Christian Reflections* and *Sermons* and (cautiously) spread the devotion to the Sacred Heart.⁵ However, during the "Papist Terror" of 1678, he was

---

³ André Ravier, "Introduction générale," in La Colombière, Écrits spirituels, 8. Ravier's introduction is my main source for La Colombière's life and spirituality.

⁴ La Colombière even recorded her account of her greatest vision in his *Spiritual Retreat of 1677*, §135 (Écrits spirituels, 165–167).

⁵ Neither the ruling Anglicanism of England nor the popular Jansenism among Catholics looked kindly on this devotion (see Ravier, "Introduction générale," in Écrits spirituels, 57).

arrested and exiled from England for the crime of being a Jesuit. His stint in prison exacerbated his already precarious health, and his last years were often spent in medically-required rest in his hometown. During a stay in Paray-le-Monial,[6] he finally succumbed to a severe hemorrhage, dying on February 15, 1682.

La Colombière's writings—all edited and published posthumously—include four volumes of *Sermons* (with a separate series of *Meditations on the Passion*), the *Christian Reflections*, two *Spiritual Retreats* and a *Spiritual Journal*, and a collection of letters. The *Retreats* and *Journal*—the first of his works to be published—were a major enkindler of devotion to the Sacred Heart.

The *Christian Reflections* are collections of passages on various topics, often serving as first drafts of passages in La Colombière's sermons. Though not written for publication, their tone is often admonitory and exhortatory,[7] very different from the intimate, self-directed tone of the *Retreats* and the *Journal*. It is in these latter

---

[6] Though his superior had been arranging his departure from the town, St. Marguerite-Marie forbid it, telling La Colombière, "He told me that He willed the sacrifice of your life in this land" (qtd. in Ravier, "Introduction générale," 65).

[7] Ravier describes their tone thus: "They represent . . . his spontaneous reaction, in some instinctive way, to the religious and moral state of the society of his times." "Introduction" to the *Christian Reflections* in Écrits spirituels, 270.

works that he shows his own spiritual ideal: that of "destruction" or, more literally, "nullification" of self in order to belong wholly to God. This ideal is perhaps better stated by Cardinal Pierre de Bérulle: man "ought to be disappropriated and nullified, and appropriated to Jesus, subsisting in Jesus, being in Jesus, living in Jesus, working in Jesus, fructifying in Jesus. . . . The life of man is to abase himself and to nullify himself in himself, to refer himself to God, to unite himself to Jesus, to live and to work in Jesus."[8]

Such "nullification"—emulating the "all-powerful and nullified God"[9]—is the spiritual ideal of La Colombière, who surrendered his own love of solitude in order to follow Jesus in the apostolic, Jesuitical life, and this "sacrifice of my heart"[10] to the Sacred Heart blossomed a fruitful tree: these *Reflections* are a bushel of its fruit.

Brandon P. Otto

---

[8] Pierre de Bérulle, *Diverse Little Works of Piety* V, in Œuvres complètes de De Bérulle, ed. Jean-Paul Migne (Paris: J. P. Migne, 1856), 914.

[9] La Colombière, *Spiritual Journal* §110, in Écrits spirituels, 147.

[10] La Colombière, *Spiritual Retreat of 1674*, §40, in Écrits spirituels, 101. This "sacrifice," specifically, is a unique vow La Colombière made to follow all the rules of the Jesuits: see *Spiritual Retreat of 1674*, §41, in Écrits spirituels, 101–8.

Note on the Text

Like all of La Colombière's writings, the *Christian Reflections* were published posthumously; the first edition was published in 1684, with slightly revised editions in 1687, 1689, and 1697. I have primarily followed the first edition of 1684, but I have occasionally used readings from the other editions (mainly the "final edition" of 1697) when there are obvious errors, though I have rarely noted it.

Of the various editions published in subsequent centuries, I have made use of two. First is a modernized edition of La Colombière's works, first published in 1757; this edition is "put in better French," as the title page says, though it also often rephrases passages and even rearranges the order of the chapters. Still, the interpretations in this edition have sometimes helped me with translating thornier passages. (A more accurate edition in 1900–1902, by Pierre Charrier, I made no use of.) Second is the 1962 edition of La Colombière's "spiritual writings" by André Ravier; though the text is almost exclusively that of the 1684 edition, Ravier's edition includes a variety of notes and, most importantly, citations for almost all of La Colombière's quotations and allusions. I have used these citations extensively, though sometimes the sources Ravier gives are either misread or simply *mal à propos* to the quotation or allusion. Still, it has been an invaluable source, especially when trying to track down quotations from excessively voluminous authors like Chrysostom and Augustine.

Except for the quotes from Epicurus in the notes to "On Conscience," all quotations in the footnotes are translated by me from the original languages. The most common source is Jean-Paul Migne's pair of enormous patristic compilations, the *Patrologia Latina* and the *Patrologia Græca*; these are cited, respectively, as PL and PG, followed by the volume number, column number, and (in most cases) column section. Thus, PL 196:327C is *Patrologia Latina*, volume 196, column 327, section C.

In translating La Colombière's text, I strove to match his style as closely as possible. All of the capitalizations found in the first edition are matched in my translation; I have only added capitalizations for pronouns referring to God or Jesus. I strove to break up La Colombière's sentences as little as possible, though

I have been liberal in rearranging punctuation to make the sentences (mostly) match English usage. However, the run-on sentence, alongside the fragmentary sentence, was common in writing of that era, and my translation reflects that.

Editions Used

Claude La Colombière. *Reflexions chrêtiennes*. Lyon: Anisson, Poseul & Rigaud, 1684.

Claude La Colombière. *Reflexions chretiennes*. Derniere edition. Lyon: Anisson & Posuel, 1697.

Claude La Colombière. *Réflexions chrétiennes sur divers sujets, et Méditations sur la Passion de N.S. Jesus-Christ*. Nouvelle Edition, mise en meilleur françois. Tome Sixieme. Lyon: Jean-Marie Bruyset, 1757.

Bienheureux Claude La Colombière. Écrits *spirituels*. Ed. André Ravier. Deuxième édition revue et augmentée. Paris: Desclée de Brouwer/Bellarmin, 1982.

Notice to the Reader[11]

After having given the Public the *Sermons*, the *Meditations on the Passion of Jesus Christ* by Père la Colombière, and his *Retreat*, the Reader will, perhaps, know how willingly I present to him a little Collection of some thoughts by the same Author. He had enough care to note down the views that came to him in the spirit, and when they appeared good and solid to him, he would give them all the space that could render them more useful to him. Afterwards, he would put them to work in his *Sermons*, as justness permitted him; for it in no way worried him to employ a good thought, as long as he believed he had found a natural and regular place for it; he was exact to the scruple, when he dealt with disposing and unifying all the parts of a discourse well.

---

[11] This notice was included in the original editions of the *Christian Reflections* but dropped in later editions. Unfortunately, the original editor of La Colombière's works did not include his name, and he remains anonymous.

One will doubtless find some of the Reflections from this Volume in his *Sermons*, but except for a few, they do not have exactly the same form. The Author had a great facility for writing well and for devoting different days to the same subject. Those who will take the pains to read this Collection with attention will draw great advantage from it: it contains a great variety of choice and remarkable things, and although some are more focused than others, they all have a befitting form which prevents one from languishing while reading them, and which, from the start, promises some profit.

On the Sweetness of Virtue

Through the practice of virtue, the passions are not destroyed, but they are tamed, which is even more useful and more agreeable. A tame Lion, elephants who fight for you, who have respect for the one who has tamed them, and who serve him as a guard and a defense. One is served by pride in despising the world, by wrath in exercising the rigors of penance against himself, with pleasure.

The world says that the yoke of Jesus Christ is unbearable, but Jesus Christ Himself says that it is sweet; the world, that His commands are difficult, but St. John: *Mandata ejus gravia non sunt [His commands are not heavy]* (1 Jn 5:3). The world—that is to say, those who do none of it—say so, but those who have tried it say the contrary: how long do we want to be blinded in this way?

The first gift God gives to the soul is His grace, with which one can do everything. The second is His love; now, love renders everything easy and agreeable. The third is an assurance of salvation, which does not permit one to doubt, which is mixed with a fear that ruins nothing. It is a light that makes one touch, that makes one feel the things of faith—a person to whom God gives this light loses, in a moment, esteem for all earthly things, and it is as if he, indeed, loses them all. It comes to him as if to a person who thought he had a million precious stones in his box, and an able jeweler made him see that these are all false jewels, that they are only glass, that they aren't worth ten écus;[12] all at once, this person, who believed himself rich, is reduced to misery, and he feels all the sorrows of poverty. This light makes him see the vanity of all that one loves upon earth, showing him their brevity, inconstancy, and unfortunate results; it makes one see the truth of all that is feared; it deals with fervor, the fear of God, and now, faith itself, which is in danger due to love of earthly things, as we have never seen an atheist or apostate who wasn't sensual, because the love and use of pleasures quenches man's spirit—and how would they

---

[12] In La Columbière's time, an écu was worth three francs.

not quench the spirit of God? They render the human spirit heavy, stupid, incapable of performing the most noble operations of its faculties and of entering into the knowledge of spiritual things. This is why naturally soft and sensual souls, if they do not do much violence to themselves, are subject to inconstancy.

Every day we see baneful proofs of this truth. What a misfortune that we let so many be carried away by love of earthly things! Let us prevent this misfortune, let us despise the sweetnesses of life, let us make this inclination to sensuality die in our heart, let us despise these passing goods, let us take our esteem and our affections away from them, let us declare ourselves against their amusements in every way, through our speech and through our actions; let us despise them, as much as our state can permit, as much as God inspires us *to do so. Sapientia hujus mundi stultitia est apud Deum [The wisdom of this world is foolishness before God]* (1 Cor 3:19).

With how much more pleasure does one walk in full day, having the end of the road before his eyes, than in the night, when he knows neither where he is nor where he is going, his faith being feeble and his spirit blind!

I will not count up all the evils from which one is delivered by practicing virtue: a woman permits herself crimes, she is satisfied, but she fears the suspicions of her husband, the infidelity of a man, confusion. Pleasures consume goods, vengeance draws forth another vengeance, etc. Beyond all that one could say of it, there is something secret, ineffable, which no tongue can express. The good have tamed passions, and being detached from the earth, they are as if armed against the disgraces and adversities that overwhelm others. Finally, try it in the name of God, since this thing is of such great consequence that, whether I deceive you or not, there is nothing but profit; if I deceive you, the worst that could happen to you would be to win heaven with pain, just like with children, when one makes them believe that the pill one gives them is a candied fruit; they swallow it, they are deceived, but they are healed.

Mihi mundus crucifixus est et ego mundo [The world is crucified to me and I to the world] (Gal 6:14). One sense of these words is this: I hold the people of the world to be very miserable, and the world regards me, in its turn, as a man to pity.

It is a greatly sorrowful matter to see so few people devoting themselves to the good, but it is strange that one does not distance oneself from it except in order to avoid sadness. One believes that it is impossible to be good and content, although, deep down, it is entirely the opposite. What deceives them is the exterior modesty of good people and their love of retreat.

All the world seeks joy in such a way that we will never draw the world to the good except in making it hope for *joy*, but how will we do this, seeing that one is warned that there is naught but crosses in the practice of virtue? As one only lets himself be drawn by joy, one does not let himself be led to prefer, to change, anything, except through a greater joy. Suppose that a soul has established its joy in loving God; it cannot fail to be eternal, since it will never discover anything that could cool its love.[13]

Although one knows that one cannot have everything—if you want pleasures, you consume your riches, you lose your reputation, you risk your life—consider this: to whom do more temporal goods remain, to libertines or to those who have embraced the party of virtue?

Saint Thomas says that the joy of the saints is like the flower of that of the blessed and that, as we have in the flower not only the hope of fruit but also a little bud, which is the beginning of the same fruit, so in

---

[13] Ravier's edition interprets this sentence as follows: "This joy cannot fail to be eternal, since this soul will never discover anything that could cool its love" (275). The original French simply has the feminine "it," and both "joy" and "soul" are feminine in French.

divine consolations, we have not only the hope of paradise but, in a way, a paradise begun.[14]

Saint Chrysostom says that all the world loves joy, that a person does not labor except for this.[15] A merchant exhausts himself in order to rejoice in his gain. A soldier risks his life for the joy that victory will bring him; a proud man seeks glory for the pleasure that he finds in enjoying this glory. Jesus Himself *preposito sibi*

---

[14] See St. Thomas Aquinas, *Commentary on Galatians*, Lecture 6, §328, on Gal 5:22: "*You have your fruit in sanctification* (Rom 6:22), that is, in sanctified works, and therefore they are called 'fruits.' They are also called 'flowers' with respect to future blessedness, since, as the hope for the fruit is received from the flowers, so, from the works of the virtues, one has the hope of eternal life and blessedness. And as, in the flower, there is a kind of beginning of the fruit, so, in the works of the virtues, there is a kind of beginning of the blessedness which there will be when knowledge and charity are perfected." Here La Colombière calls holy men and women on earth "saints," while those in heaven, who enjoy the beatific vision, are "the blessed."

[15] See St. John Chrysostom, *Homilies to the People of Antioch, on the Statues* XVIII.1: "For everyone desires pleasure and rejoicing, and, because of this, everyone does and says and works. And so the merchant sails for this, in order to gather goods; so he gathers goods in order that, having a reserve, he might rejoice; and the soldier soldiers for this, and the farmers farms for this, and each plies his trade for this, and the lovers of power love for this, so that they might enjoy glory, and they want to enjoy glory, so that they might rejoice" (PG 49:181).

gaudio sustinuit crucem [having set joy before Himself, endured the Cross] (Heb 12:2). Saint Augustine approves Virgil's saying, *trahit sua quemque voluptas [his desire draws each one on]*.[16] In effect, if one asks each one what he desires, all would respond, says St. Augustine, *velle gaudere [that he wants to rejoice]*.[17]

No one in the party of good people has ever complained about not being content; in the other *party*, Solomon himself, the most fortunate of all men, recognizes that all is naught but vanity and affliction of spirit (Eccl 1:14).[18]

Virtue raises us above men, which is why one owes respect, a sincere respect, to good people, in contrast

---

[16] Virgil, *Eclogue* II.65, quoted in St. Augustine, *Tractates on the Gospel of St. John* XXVI.4: "Further, if poets are allowed to say 'his desire draws each one on'—not necessity, but desire; not obligation, but delight—how much more are we *allowed* to say that we ought to draw to Christ a man who delights in truth, who delights in beatitude, who delights in justice, who delights in eternal life, which is the whole Christ?" (PL 35:1608).

[17] See St. Augustine, *Confessions* X.XXI.31: "For though, perhaps, one delights in this, one in that, yet all agree that they want to be blessed, inasmuch as they would agree, if they were asked, that they want to rejoice, and they call this joy 'the blessed life'" (PL 32:793).

[18] "Affliction of spirit" is a literal translation of the Vulgate's form of this verse, *universa vanitas et afflictio spiritus*. Most translations instead read "striving after wind," though the Douay-Rheims has "vexation of spirit."

to sinners, to whom one renders *respect* only by force. One respects the former in their absence; the latter are torn apart everywhere that they are not.

The same honors are more honorable for good people, since they are the fruits of their merit; instead, with the others, they serve only to make one notice their vices, and to make one remember their artifices, violences, injustices, and perfidies through which they attained them.

We have a great interest in being on good terms with Him Who distributes all goods, but God does not give prosperity to His friends. He must distinguish when adversities are necessary for them, but when they make so good a use of goods that instead of being attached to the world, they regard nothing but eternity, God covers them with all kinds of disgraces. He favors the wicked, that's true, when He wants to lose them, yet this is not for a long time, for fear of scandalizing the others, and to repair this apparent injustice and to justify His conduct, He permits sudden deaths, *permits* that their children be miserable, that a trial ruin them: a disgrace despoils them of everything, and no one has compassion on them.

Men can do good to us, be it because they esteem us, be it because they love us, be it because they love themselves, for their own interests. For one does not love, one does not esteem, one does not hope except for the esteem and friendship of good men; vice is not esteemed, and reasonably, for what mediator trusts the vicious? What salutary counsel can one expect from such people who counsel themselves so poorly? What profit comes from their friendship, which is ordinarily more feared than their hatred? Do you base yourself on their credit? It is not trusted. It would be a great recklessness to take as surety the word of a person who can't keep it before God.

Debauches consume the good and hinder one from acquiring it, ruin one's honor and health, distance one from jobs and duties; one wouldn't dare to entrust a considerable affair to a vicious man; when one recognizes a man in disorder, one avoids him: one would say that the very sight of him is contagious. That one could, indeed, accept the promise of a man who has no other rule or other measure than his pleasure! We see that even the vicious want no one but good men, women, domestic servants, workers; one always prefers those of whose probity one is sure, for they fear God.

In vain, one tells men that the goods down here are nothing, exaggerating their vanity, comparing them to eternal ones, and making whole books in order to point out the difference between them. Job says in vain that all human happiness is only a speck.[19] It is true that they are short, bounded, deceiving, these pleasures, but they are sensible, one sees them, and the others are invisible. One is astonished that reasonable men would not want to take the effort to consider these truths, that, after having recognized their vanity through their own experience, they are still attached to them—but here is a cause for much greater astonishment, which is that everyone professing to only care for temporal interests, sacrificing religion, repose, health, etc. for them, they do not see that one does not find them except in the practice of virtue, or though seeing this, they do not embrace it.

One cannot doubt that God is the author of all goods, even temporal, of which vice, which distances us from God, deprives us. What misery to separate oneself from God for the sake of goods that one cannot receive except from Him, to renounce virtue for reasons which ought to attach us to it, to lose eternity, to run after a happiness that one cannot find except in seeking eternity itself!

---

[19] Perhaps a reference to the Vulgate of Job 21:13: "They spend their days among goods, and, in a moment, they descend to hell." The Vulgate's Latin for "in a moment" is *in puncto*, recalling La Colombière's phrasing here, that human happiness *n'est qu'une point*.

On Desires

The felicity of the other life is the accomplishment of all desires. The felicity of this life is the nullification of all desires. To be happy in this world, one must desire none of all the things in this world: *Imperavit ventis, et facta est tranquillita magna*, "He appeased the winds, and all was calm" (Mt 8:26).

The only happiness in this life is to not establish one's happiness here, to be persuaded that one cannot be happy here.

Desires grow in the measure that we obtain what we have desired; the possession of what we have hoped for does nothing but nourish desires without satiating the soul. The soul desires naught but this charge,[20] since

---

[20] La Colombière frequently uses the word "charge" to refer to an official position one has been granted, an official duty. In his time, being a government officer was considered a great bestower of status, and the higher the office, the greater the status. In the *Reflections*, he frequently speaks of this pride-driven desire to move up the officials ranks by gaining ever greater charges.

it is persuaded, seduced by the senses and by the false opinions of men, that this charge will satisfy it, but seeing that this is naught but a drop of water in an abyss, it is drawn to other objects, which the senses also represent to it as goods capable of fulfilling it.

The wicked rich man asked for nothing but a drop of water (Lk 16:24): this was his whole desire; I leave you to think if this would have quenched his thirst; he will not have it, but if he had it, etc.

If we had the fulfillment of all our desires in this life, we would no longer think of the other, and thus God, Who loves us, arranges things differently. God has made a decree of His providence: will you change it? But the reprobates, are they subject to this law? Yes, to avoid scandal. This is why God often permits those *who are* happy in this world to die at a just time, when their good fortune seems to have risen to its summit, and when they have nothing more to enjoy here: these are victims whom He has fattened, it seems, only in order to immolate them for public instruction. This has even passed into a Proverb, so often does it happen: "when the nest is complete, the bird flies away."

There is a malady one dies from, which is an excess of health. These are our desires, which consume us and which use up our health through the cares that they bring to birth, the fatigues that they make us bear, which is why it happens that many die, since they had obtained what they desired.

One obtains nothing without much labor, because of the multitude of pretenders; each wants to draw fortune to himself in such a way that each of those who desire to enrich themselves have to fight all the others.

The majority of the time, one obtains nothing, or at the least, one obtains little; never does one obtain all that one wants. What grief to be frustrated by one's desires and by the fruit of such fatigues!

Desires are always accompanied by fear, and fear is the greatest of all evils.

An author says that a man who has many desires is like a poor mother who sees herself surrounded by children who ask for bread and who do not have it; what pain to thus seem them die of hunger!

Ordinarily, our desires hinder each other: the desire for glory and for life, for good and for repose, for reputation and for pleasure. One must, by necessity, risk the one in pursuing the other, and thus, there is a double pain: impatience, disquiet, the fatigues that one must overcome in order to attain what one yearns for, and the fear of losing what one wants to preserve, the fear of losing honor without having this pleasure.

The prodigal child, *Et cupiebat implere ventrem suum de siliquis, quas porci manducabant, et nemo illi dabat [And he desired to fill his belly with the pods which the pigs ate, and no one gave* them *to him]* (Lk 15:16). Behold how strange it is that he only wanted to be satisfied with a pod, and yet he does not find one; if it was exotic foods, etc. How unfortunate you are: how many servants of God live contented in their poverty while you die of hunger in the midst of the goods that surround you!

It is the same with earthly riches as with human knowledge; a man who knows little and who has no curiosity is easily persuaded that he is knowledgeable, but those whom desire for learning leads to see all, to read all, to penetrate all, always become more ignorant in their own opinion, and day by day, they are more persuaded of their ignorance; they find, after all this, that they know nothing. Just the same, although through a very different cause, a man who has no cupidity, although he has only a few goods, is easily contented, and he does not find that he is lacking anything, while a man possessed by avarice, the more he acquires, the more he sees that he is indigent; his needs grow with his riches, all his acquisitions only make him know his poverty and the insatiability of his desires.

On Desires

A man is in bed, belabored by an ardent fever, which causes an extreme alteration in him; one can extinguish his thirst in two ways: by giving him cold water to drink in some quantity, which would entirely quench him, or by taking away the fever which causes this alteration in him, for, the cause being removed, the effect ceases. If one would give this sick man the choice of one or the other of these two remedies, who would doubt that he would much more prefer that one cure him of the fever instead of only giving him water to drink? For even though, after he has drunk with excess, it happens that the thirst comes to cease, if it is so that the fever is always remaining, it will begin again forthwith.

Adam and Eve imagined that they were as happy as God when they knew good and evil; the demon made them understand that they had only to eat of the forbidden fruit in order to have this knowledge, and he did not deceive them; they had it by this means, but very far from rendering them happier than they were before, it served only to cover them with confusion and to make them fall into all the evils of which it gave them knowledge.

The mere desire for a thing is very often an obstacle to obtaining it. The reason is that desire blinds and makes you lose that cold sense which is so necessary for success. One sees an example of this in persons who have a great desire to please: these are, ordinarily, those who render themselves ridiculous by a thousand forced manners, and full of affectation, who render themselves obnoxious through their importunate chatter, through their importunate civility. Where do you think this hindrance comes from, this which sometimes appears in certain persons who otherwise have merit? It could be the effect of a bad education or of a natural timidity, but take away the desire to please: you will take away the fear of committing faults and, at the same time, the source of the greatest follies that one customarily commits in civil life. One is ridiculous less due to bad qualities than due to the good ones that one affects.

What ruined that merchant? The too-great desire of enriching himself; he ran risks on all sides, etc. A shipwreck, a bankruptcy, etc. He plundered all hands, etc. It befell him as *it befalls* those who still want to eat after they are full: they reject both the superfluous and the necessary.

Concupiscence has the same effect in the rich as necessity in the poor; these are two leeches that cry out without cease, "give, give": *Sanguisugæ duæ sunt filiæ dicentes affer affer [Two are the daughters of the leech, saying, "Bring, bring"]* (Prv 30:15).

The first pain of the man who desires is the desire *itself*; the labor, the lowness to which one is reduced in order to satisfy it, even unto keeping pigs. The obstacle to the desire, the augmentation of the desire by the obstacle itself, frustration of the desire by the desire itself, by other desires, by other desirers.

All that you desire cannot make you happy, and it can make you unhappy.

The desired thing, instead of satisfying desire, augments it; first, one desires only a little bit of a common thing, the acquisition of which is easy; you have obtained it; it produces the desire for rare things, great things, things difficult to acquire. Not only does the remedy not cure, but it augments the ill.

Desire is the love of an absent good; it is a movement of the soul, says Philo,[21] by which it stretches out

---

[21] See Philo of Alexandria, *On the Special Laws* IV.79: "Every passion is censurable, since every measureless and excessive impulse and *every* irrational and unnatural movement of the soul is culpable." See *Philo*, Volume VIII, ed. and tr. F. H. Colson (Cambridge, MA: Harvard University Press, 1999), 56. See also Philo, *Who Is the Heir of Divine Things*, §269: "For when desire rules, there arises a yearning for absent things, and it hangs the soul as if from a noose of unfulfilled hope." See *Philo*, Volume IV, ed. and tr. F. H. Colson and G. H. Whitaker (Cambridge, MA: Harvard University Press, 1958), 420.

in order to be able to reach what it loves, because of which it is enfeebled, it is discovered, it suffers.

Saint Thomas, after Aristotle, says that there are two kinds of desires: a natural desire and a reasonable one.[22] Saint Chrysostom, after Plato, calls the first necessary and the second unnecessary.[23] The natural, says Aristotle, is bounded; the reasonable is infinite.[24] The reason that he gives it is that its object is the end of man, which one never stops seeking.

---

[22] See St. Thomas Aquinas, *Summa Theologiæ* I–II, q. 30, a. 3: "The first natural desires are common to men and to the other animals.... But the second desires are proper to men.... Wherefore the Philosopher also says that the first desires are irrational, while the second are with reason. And since diverse things are reasoned about in diverse manners, so the second are also called 'proper and apposite,' that is, beyond the natural." St. Thomas is referencing Aristotle's *Rhetoric* I.11 and *Nicomachean Ethics* III.11.

[23] Plato's distinction of necessary and unnecessary desires is found in the *Republic*, Book VIII (558ff). Condemnation of unnecessary desires, goods, and wealth is endemic in Chrysostom's writings; one good example is his *Homilies on Ephesians*, Homily II, where he details how sins arise from going beyond the bounds of necessity, while what is necessary is not sinful.

[24] I have not found such a distinction in Aristotle's discussions of desire in general, but it appears, in a different form, in his discussion of wealth, where he distinguishes between a "natural art of acquisition," limited by the specific needs of a household, and a limitless "wealth-getting"; see *Politics* I.8–9.

Richard of Saint Victor compares the heart of man to an abyss, and all the world to a morsel, based on these words: *Dilata os tuum, et implebo illud [Open up your mouth, and I will fill it]* (Ps 81:10).[25] You want to be satisfied: either desire less or desire more. You want to be fulfilled at once: either be content with little or let nothing content you but God. Plato causes desire to be born from abundance and from necessity.

The fire is kindled in the measure that it has what it seems to desire. Our desires are like fire: the more one gives them, the more they grow.

The emperor-philosopher Marcus Aurelius Antoninus, in his *Philosophy*, says, "I frankly confess here, and although *it is* to my confusion, I will not stop saying it for the instruction of ages to come, that in the space of fifty years, which I have lived, I wanted to test how far vice can go in this life, to see if the passions have bounds, and after a long and serious research, I find that the more I eat, the more hungry I am; the more I drink, the more thirsty I am. If I sleep too much, I want to sleep still

---

[25] See Richard of St. Victor, *Mystical Annotations on the Psalms*, Annotation on Psalm LXXX: "What a morsel is to the mouth of the flesh, such—rather, much less—is the whole world to the mouth of the heart. For a bodily morsel easily fills a mouth, but the whole world is not enough to fulfill the desire of the heart" (PL 196:327C).

more; the more rest I take, the more fatigued and ill I feel; the more I have, the more, too, I desire to have; the more I amass, the less, too, I possess; in a word, I obtain nothing that does not forthwith annoy me; I immediately turn away and desire something else."[26]

In this life, the more things one hopes for, the more one has to fear from them, and thus one cannot be happy; in the measure that one possesses what one desires, one feels both desires and fear increase: the more one has, the more one desires, the more one fears.

God threatens, as if it were a great evil, to leave the sinner prey to his desires: *Famem patientur ut canes, et circuibunt civitatem [They shall suffer hunger like dogs, and they shall go round about the city]* (Ps 59:6); after having amassed silver, one wants to buy houses, lands, loads of goods.

To be happy in this life, it is necessary that God be all in all things for us, as He will be in the other *life*. Those who were disgusted by manna were those for whom it did not have all tastes, *Deus meus et omnia [My God and all]*.[27]

---

[26] This passage is not found in any of Marcus Aurelius's writings or in any fragments attributed to him.

[27] This is the motto of St. Francis of Assisi and, thus, of the various Franciscan orders. On the idea of manna having all tastes, see Ws 16:21; on disgust at the manna, see Nm 11:4–6.

One desires the things of this world with ardor, but one possesses them without pleasure; one has no joy from them. "I had to rejoice," says the Father of the prodigal child, "since I recovered a lost child, but that you are always with me, this is not a joy which is sensible to me" (Lk 15:31–32). The loss of a sheep can well cause a mortal affliction in the shepherd, but the possession of the ninety-nine is not a good which is sensible to him (Lk 15:1–7).

The reason why one is never content is that one does not reflect on what one has but on what one does not have; "one does not regard," says St. Basil, "an infinite number of persons who are poorer: one has his eyes on the one who is richer than us;"[28] one does completely the opposite with regard to spiritual goods, for which one is less avid; one considers those who have less virtue: *Gratias tibi ago, quod non sum sicut cæteri hominum, raptores, injusti, adulteri, velut etiam hic publicanus [I give You thanks that I not like the rest of men, thieves, unjust, adulterers, or even like this publican]* (Lk 18:11). One regards what one has acquired, *jejuno bis in Sabbato, etc. [I fast twice a week, etc.]* (Lk 18:12), which is why one is soon content with oneself and with

---

[28] See St. Basil the Great, *Homily to the Rich*, §5 (PG 31:292B–296A). La Colombière is summarizing Basil's argument, not giving his exact words.

one's virtue; instead, one must cast one's eyes upon what we lack, and this would kindle within us a holy ardor to better ourselves.

God, having made us for Himself, our heart necessarily goes to Him and as if by instinct; one cannot prevent this; one can well deceive *the heart* and propose to it, as its sovereign good, a fragile good and one which passes away, but the effort one makes in going further, the disgust that one conceives of it, or the hunger that still remains in him for a much greater good, make him see that he has not found what he was looking for.

Ite Angeli veloces ad gentem expectantem et conculcatam [Go, swift Angels, to the expectant and downtrodden people] (Is 18:2), that is to say, to those persons full of vain desires and still vainer hopes, *expectantem [expectant]*, and who, in order to not lose them, suffer the disdain and the rebukes of the great ones of the earth, *et conculcatam [and downtrodden]*.

Is it in this world that we come to that true happiness? The pleasures of the world which first satisfy us, its honors, its glory, and its riches which never satisfy, all its false goods, by which some are disgusted, and for which others hunger, which all pass away like smoke, and whose use is always troubled by a mixture of infinite evils, and by the terrible image of death, where they will all finally end—can they produce this happiness?

God has two sovereignties: the one consists in possessing Himself, in being independent of every created being, in needing nothing; the other belongs to Him with regard to creatures, over whom He has an absolute dominion and whom He can dispose of. The man who wants to be like God can resemble Him, in some way, through the first of these two sovereignties, which forms God's happiness, which makes Him God, and seek to resemble Him in the other, which is not able to render us happy, and which is itself founded upon the first, without which it would be impossible; this is why a man who does not possess himself is the slave of creatures rather than their master.

After having used up health in order to acquire goods, one will have to consume those goods in order to recover health; one has to taste pleasures to content nature; one must abstain from them to conserve it.

A single desire excites all the passions, and it is impossible that you will not be exposed to the tyranny of all those ferocious beasts if you give yourself as prey to a single desire. This is why Saint Paul has said, *Radix malorum cupiditas [The root of evils is cupidity]* (1 Tm 6:10).

Saint Chrysostom, explaining the words *Panem nostrum quotidianum [Our daily bread]* (Mt 6:11), says: "Note how much virtue He wants in us in that which regards the body; for He does not command us to ask Him for riches, or for pleasures, or for costly clothes, or anything similar, but only for bread, and for the bread we need on the day in which we are living, without us making pains about tomorrow."[29]

---

[29] See St. John Chrysostom, *Homilies on the Gospel of Matthew*, 19.5 (PG 57:280). Some English translations have different section numbers, so that this passage is instead in *Homilies on Matthew* 19.8.

On Faith

All faithlessness is not only in the understanding, it is also in the will. The reason why one does not believe is because one does not want to believe. To believe, say the Theologians, there must be a pious movement of the will which bends the understanding; it is true that one must believe in order to love, but it is no less true that one must love in order to believe well: *Charitas omnia credit [Charity believes all things]* (1 Cor 13:7).

All Catholics believe, but it is very necessary that all believe in the same way.[30] It is not the little-illuminated or too-illuminated understanding, the most ignorant women, the most knowing Doctors *which causes faith*. It was not the hindrance of spirit nor custom in Saint Paul and in Saint Augustine, it was not despair nor necessity in Saint Henry, nor in Constantine, it was

---

[30] The original edition read "that all do not believe in the same way," but later editions dropped the "not."

not timidity nor feebleness of spirit in Saint Louis nor in Charlemagne.

It is not reason which is the cause of incredulity in man, since one has never seen a man of good sense doubt the things of religion if he was not corrupted in his manners.

Why is it that, of all the heretics, not one of good faith is converted who was not prepared for this grace by an innocent and regulated life, and that one has never seen an apostate Catholic who was not, furthermore, a very bad Christian? Why is it that the Church is never abandoned except by children who dishonor her and whom she has to cut off, herself, from her mystical body, and that, on the contrary, no new subject comes to us from the side of our enemies who was not the glory of his party and who did not live as if he were already faithful?

Faith supposes two habits, or rather, it is composed of them: one in the understanding, the other in the will. It is necessary that the understanding know and that the will love the truths of the faith in order to believe them. How will we know them if we neglect to instruct ourselves? How will we love them if we preserve in ourselves the passions that they fight?

You do not have that faith which the saints had? God has not given it to you? But you have asked it from Him for so long? What alms, what vows, what prayers have you made to obtain it? To what saint have you addressed yourself? It is only God alone Who can give it to you; it is thus necessary to ask it from Him, with insistence, to push Him, to importune Him, *Domine ut videam [Lord, that I might see]* (Lk 18:41). You do not have that living faith, those supernatural lights that would reveal to the spirit the most impenetrable mysteries and would sweeten for the soul that which appears most bitter by nature. I am not astonished at this: and where would you have drawn these lights from: from the alleys, from the impious and licentious conversations that one had in the world today, from the poisoned books that nourish your passions and poison your heart?

Why is it that that Christian who believes feebly, who, however, makes profession of so strict a morality, digs through all the glosses of Scripture in order to impose upon his neighbor an indispensable obligation to not draw any profit from his silver, does not merely reflect upon the so natural, so visible obligation that he has to employ his revenues in order to adorn the altars and dress the poor, who are the living temples of the Holy Spirit? God has said in the Gospel that one must have pity on the poor, that it was He Whom one succors in their person (Mt 25:34–40). That lady who is so liberal by her nature and who has a tender and compassionate heart takes no pains to believe that the Son of God is present to her in the person of the miserable. But He said that the time is short, that one must employ it well, that one will demand an account from us of all moments: why is it that she does not listen to this truth and that she gambles from morning to evening? It is because she loves games, and because this truth shocks that inclination. For this rich man, there is no severe enough opinion against profusion and luxury, but also no formal enough text in the Scripture, no eloquent enough place in the Fathers, in favor of almsgiving. Preach to that young man respect for the Body of Jesus Christ; it is a marvel how much of an impression you will make upon his spirit; he will be terrified by the very name of sacrilege, he will spend whole years without approaching the sacraments, he will declaim against frequent Communions, and he will say upon this point more than the most austere reformers of Christian morality, but why is it that this same man, to whom faith gives so penetrating a sight, so profound a respect, even so ardent a zeal, has no faith for those terrible worlds: *Neque adulteri, neque molles [Neither adulterers, nor the effeminate]* (1 Cor 6:9), etc. Why is it that he lacks respect for his own body, which is the very body of Jesus Christ, according to Saint Paul (1 Cor 12:27), and that he even dares to take the members of the Savior in order to prostitute them to prostituted women (1 Cor 6:15)? Why is it that he, this severe doctor, is indulgent with regard to those who are culpable of this crime, unto excusing their greatest disorders, unto supposing an indispensable necessity to sin in them; why is it, I say, that there are truths which painlessly enter into his heart, and others which find no point of access there, that is, those find no passions in us which are contrary to them, and the others shock our bad inclinations, our bad habits? *Beati mundo corde, quoniam ipsi Deum videbunt [Blessed are the pure of heart, for they shall see God]* (Mt 5:8). They shall see God in this life; they shall see the truth of all things.

There is an error among Christian men: it is that faith is such a gift from God that it is not in their power to acquire it, or to fortify it, even when they easily agree that they have little of it, and even claim to excuse themselves, due to this default of faith and intelligence, for all the other disorders of their life. Why is it that, although one often reproaches them for their little faith, they are no more touched by it than if one told them that they do not have the gift of miracles? They admire this virtue in the saints as a purely gratuitous gift; they persuade themselves that one forces himself to increase his faith in vain, that it is necessary to wait in idleness for God to grant them this favor, that one would make efforts to believe in vain, and that there is no means to attain it. "I am well aware that faith is feeble in me, but, although I greatly force myself to have a most vivid one, I am well aware that this is not in my power. I hope for the lights of those saints who painlessly detached themselves from all that is not God, but what does it serve me to desire it if God has not resolved to give them to me?" It is necessary to disabuse ourselves and to see whose fault it is that we do not believe, that it is ourselves, that, whatever we might say, we do not believe, because we do not want to believe.

The wicked and corrupted will destroys God as much as is possible for it, that is to say, it destroys Him in the spirit and in the belief of man. Why is it that a humble God, that a tender and merciful God, a God *Who is* charitable even unto becoming man, appears to you as a chimera, while a lax and vindictive God, a deceitful and adulterous God, a God *who is* immodest even unto changing himself into a beast in order to satisfy a brutal passion, finds an infinity of adorers in paganism:[31] is it because he is more realistic? It is because those pagans loved vengeance and adultery and because you are horrified by humility.

Faith was free in the prisons of the first Christians; it is enchained and captive since they became free. There is faith in you; you might well have been an atheist and an unbeliever; it is true that faith is captive within you, but the efforts it makes to deliver itself, the frights that it gives your conscience from time to time, those doubts that you propose to yourself at every moment regarding the matter of common belief, make you see that you are very far from that calm and from that tranquility which a total and perfect persuasion is wont to produce. One might say that you are seeking the resolution of your doubts, although, in truth, you seek only to confirm yourself in your error, through the sentiment of judicious persons whom you believe ought to enter into your sentiments. You are seeking what you hope you will not find.

Why is it that one believes at the hour of death? It is because one has lost even hope for all the things of the world, it is because the veil is broken, it is because the

---

[31] This was a common practice of Zeus in Greek and Roman mythology.

passions are extinguished; one sees the despairing, but few atheists.

Why this extreme negligence of the things relating to your salvation? "It is because I do not believe that my soul is immortal"—that is not it: you are very persuaded that your body is mortal, and you do not stop yourself from taking extreme care of it and embellishing it with all that is most exquisite and most brilliant in art and nature; it is because you love only dirt and dung.

It is strange that, notwithstanding everyday experience, one takes all the pains in the world to persuade men that they must die; one sees that, at twenty-four years, they believe themselves very far from the tomb; the doctors have declared the ruling of death, and they have drawn away, the confessor cries in the sick man's ears that there is time to think of departure, and he still cannot be persuaded that he is going to die, because he cannot resolve himself to it, since he hopes that his body is immortal; on the contrary, one cannot believe the soul immortal, since one hopes that it will die with the body.

When the heart has prevented *faith*, in vain does one enlighten the understanding; the Jews are a great proof of this: the parables, which render the highest mysteries sensible, were for them impenetrable veils which concealed them from their sight. Had they not seen the miracles, had they not themselves avowed that He had done a great number of them, *Quia hic homo multa signa facit [For this man does many signs]* (Jn 11:47)? And yet they concluded that it was necessary to promptly put Him to death.

The Jews wanted to be informed about the man born blind; they called the parents, they were convinced, they overlooked nothing in order to seduce him; the fruit: did they believe? They cursed him, they insulted him, they excommunicated him (Jn 9:13–34).

A passion in the heart which relaxation and laziness have already softened is like a fire that attaches itself to a wet matter; it excites a thick smoke which blinds reason and hinders it from seeing supernatural things. Passion renders us blind with regard even to sensible things: must it be astonishing if it conceals the knowledge of spiritual and divine things from us? That which rejects the wicked, draws the good; that which causes pain to the libertines, consoles good people. They cannot admire enough what others cannot believe: the Eucharist, the Incarnation, the death of a God, which exercises the faith of wicked Christians, does nothing but further inflame the love of the most regulated and the most serving *Christians*. If you speak of the nullification of a God in His incarnation, one must be blind, they will say, to believe in so prodigious an abasement. One must be more insensible than rocks to not be touched by so perfect and so extraordinary a love: "how can we believe all these miracles?" say the libertines, hearing talk of the Holy Sacrament. How artful is Your love, how inventive it is, how tender it is, how worthy it is of all our love! "There are none but simpletons and idiots who could believe this Miracle," says an ignorant man who lives in disorder, when he understands the marvels which God has operated in His people's favor, and which He still does every day to glorify His saints. "How admirable is God in His saints,"[32] says that other man, illumined by lights, who is drawn by the subjection of his passions and by the regulation of his life. *Vere non est alius Deus, nisi Deus noster [Truly, there is no other God except our God]*, etc.

Your *Credo* rebukes you, and it would convert the peoples of India and Japan. "Is not all this incredible?" you say. "Is not all this very lovable," say those Pagans, "and all together very reasonable? Is this not the most powerful and, at the same time, the best of all the Gods?"

---

[32] This is the Vulgate version of Ps 68:35.

Tertullian has said that the soul is naturally Christian[33] in order to make us understand that if we do not believe, it is an effect of corruption. Where could this come from? Would it not be from the simplicity, the ignorance, or the prejudice of those who believe? One might think so, if Saint Paul (Rom 1:19–20), Saint Denis,[34] Saint Augustine[35] did not find themselves of the same sentiment as the simpletons and the idiots.

Of all states, the most miserable is that of a Christian who believes little; it would be better to believe nothing, since he suffers more in his pleasures than a

---

[33] See Tertullian, *Apology*, §17: "O testimony of the naturally Christian soul!" (PL 1:377A).

[34] Pseudo-Dionysius the Areopagite, in his *On the Divine Names*, mentions how we can know God through the arrangement of the universe (VII.3; PG 3:869D–872A); however, he also talks about God's foolish, non-rational Wisdom (VII.1; PG 3:868A); it is "non-rational" because it is so far above reason (VII.2; PG 3:869A); thus those who believe are often considered to be mad and irrational, while they have actually reached the supra-rational truth (VII.4; PG 3:872D–873A).

[35] See St. Augustine, *On the Spirit and the Letter*, XII.19–20: "See how he does not call them ignorant of the truth, but *he says* that they hold on to truth in iniquity . . . for he says that, through visible creatures, they come to the knowledge of the invisible Creator . . . to those knowing the Creator through the creature, that same knowledge profits them nothing for salvation, *since, knowing God, they have not glorified Him as God, or given thanks, saying that they themselves are wise* (Rom 10:3)" (PL 44:212–213).

truly faithful person in his cruelest pains; this bit of light that remains in him suffices to lose him, and it does not suffice to save him. His faith is an importune light, and as if a false ray, which takes away the repose one tastes in the darkness, without giving them the joy that belongs to the day, like a sick man for whom there remains enough force to feel the suffering of his ill, but too little to surmount it.

It is, however, useless to make Christians recognize that they are little firm in their belief; they recognize it enough, they feel it, they even avow it without blushing, they even claim to excuse themselves for this default, since they judge all the deregulations of their life involuntary, they complain about it, they hope to be enlightened, since they are persuaded that the light which would reveal the truth of the mysteries to them would facilitate the observation of the commandments in them, and that it would be easy enough for them to practice the Gospel, which is difficult for them to believe.

The gift of intelligence, which dissipates the doubts and darkness of the spirit, which makes one believe with joy and makes the spirit submit itself, without pain, to the obscurest truths, this admirable quality which makes us penetrate into the most profound mysteries, which makes us see what is most hidden in the conduct of God, which reveals to us the reasons for things which are most elevated above reason, which even appear most contrary to it—in a word, this precious gift which calms the disquiet of our spirit, and which fortifies our faith at a point when miracles are useless to us, and when one is no less persuaded by what one believes than by what one sees: this intelligence, I say, is poured out in our hearts with sanctifying grace, and, as it is born and dies with it, so does it regulate its increases based on its augmentations; now, as it is in our power to augment grace in ourselves, so it is *in our power* to fortify faith through good works.

"I would immediately quit these pleasures if I had faith," and I myself tell you that you will immediately have faith once you have quit these pleasures. It happens every day that one employs very useless remedies against the infidels, since one applies them where there is no ill; the ill is in the heart, and not in the spirit; one believes that it is error, and it is passion, and one uses long reasonings.

Of the two birds which Noah made depart from the ark, which was the figure of the Church, the dove, finding no place to stop, returned to the ark; the raven would have done the same without that brutal avidity which brought it to attach itself to a floating cadaver in order to feed itself (Gn 8:6–9). It can happen that a chaste soul sometimes wanders into doubts which the weakness of his spirit, or the malignity of the demon, arouses in it, but as it has no passion to sustain its weakness, it always returns to the Spirit, while a black soul, and plunged into vice, is seized by the filthy delights which creatures present to it. The heretics understood this truth; this is why they have all begun by seducing the will, not doubting that it would drag the understanding into the most ridiculous errors and the most opposed to common sense.

Faith has been given to supplement reason, to elevate us above reason. Why is it that it aids reason rather than being aided by it?

On Conscience

Conscience is the voice of God; in the majority of men, this voice is either despised or poorly understood, or entirely snuffed out. It is despised in those who want to do nothing it says, poorly understood in those who make it say all that they want, snuffed out in those who despise it without receiving reproach from it. The last of these states is, doubtless, the worst, because it is not at all easy to leave it, since it is a despaired state, but the others lead to this, and, apart from the fact that one leaves them more easily than the last, one could say that they are worse: the last is the punishment for the others.

One despises this voice—that is the first step; it warns us of the evil we have done, of that which we ought to avoid, of the good we could do; for each time we obey, how many times do we despise this voice? Yet it is the voice of reason, it is the voice of man, it is our own judgment, it is what we consider most reasonable. This is why God will not condemn us except on the basis of the judgment that we have, ourselves, made of ourselves: it is the voice of grace, this advice, this good counsel you receive in the depths of your heart, it is the price of the Blood of Jesus Christ, it is the seed of eternity, it is the voice of the Holy Spirit.

This disdain can oblige this friend to be silent, and even to change its friendship into hate and into fury. When this friend speaks, it speaks all; when it no longer speaks all, it is silent. The man is as if in a lethargy, the interior senses no longer acting; all the others no longer function. To draw us away from this, one must apply iron and fire, humiliation, shameful falls, etc.

One afflicts this friend; see the disquiet, the bitterness that rests in the heart of a man who takes hold of a pleasure against his conscience; I speak of a man whose conscience is not yet mute; the joy of a man who has obeyed his conscience, which commanded him to pardon, to restore another's good, to do a good work, a giving of alms, a general confession, after having lived, I do not say in crime, but in looseness and in tepidity, who was wrapped up, for some time, in things which he finally recognized as being wicked, who, for many years, permitted himself dangerous attachments, scarcely Christian vanities, vengeances, resentments, calumnies, who sees that his confessions were without contrition, that he went to them as if he were going to make or receive a visit, that he told his sins in nearly the same manner as one tallies an account, that his communions were without preparation, without devotion, without fruit, that he went to them as if by habit, for human respect, by force, etc. When one has vanquished a human respect, one has sacrificed an interest.

It is necessary to content the conscience, when it speaks to us, in order to not oblige it to cry out and to trouble our repose, in order to not oblige it to keep silent, and leave you in a mortal drowsiness.

In whatever state you are, even in prosperity. For, in adversity, the conscience is crueler than ever; often this wakes it up, since, being rejected by creatures, one returns to faith.

Jussisti Domine, et sic est, ut pœna sibi sit omnis inordinatus animus [You have ordered, Lord, and so it is, that every disordered soul shall be a punishment to itself], says Saint Augustine.[36] This is just, and this is the Divine Providence which regulated things in such a way that, as, in sinning, we violate three kinds of laws—that of reason, human law, and divine law—so it is just that we

---

[36] See St. Augustine, *Confessions*, I.XII.19 (PL 32:670).

would suffer three kinds of pains, and that we would be punished by ourselves, through the reproaches of our conscience, by men, through temporal pains, and by God, through eternal ones.

That man who comes to will that there were no God is a man whom God pursues everywhere, who is importuned by Him. But does he come to the point of believing in Him? I challenge that. The most that he could do is to doubt. But what cruel doubt! A man on trial, whatever good right he has, cannot stop from trembling, but if he has a thousand witnesses against him, if he has no one in his part except some wicked, corrupt judges, etc.

"The sinner," says St. John Chrysostom,[37] "always has fear; he fears everything, down to his shadow; the least noise frightens him, and he imagines that all those around him are thinking of some reason against him. If one speaks of him in secret, it is about one of his crimes that they converse. The sinner reveals himself, although no one accuses him; he trembles, although there is no appearance of danger. Hear in what way the Holy Spirit describes this fear of sinners and the assurance of the just: *Fugit peccator nemine persequente*

---

[37] See St. John Chrysostom, *Homilies to the People of Antioch, on the Statues*, VIII.1–2 (PG 49:99).

[The sinner flees, none pursuing] (Prv 28:1), and why does he flee, no one pursuing him? Because, in his own conscience, he has an accuser who gives him no respite, and whom he always carries with him, and as he cannot flee from himself, he cannot evade this pursuer, who follows him everywhere, beating him, whipping him, and causing him incurable wounds, but the just man is not so: *Justus confidit ut leo [The just man trusts like the lion]* (Prv 28:1)." *Finis autem præcepti est charitas in corde puro, et conscientia bona [But the end of the law is charity in a pure heart and a good conscience]* (1 Tm 1:5). "He adds, *conscientia bona [good conscience]*," says St. Augustine, "because of hope, since he who has the witness of a bad conscience within himself despairs of attaining what he believes in."[38] The hope of each one is in his own conscience, in the measure that one feels filled with the love of God.

The Apostle demands a clear conscience in order to establish hope, since only he who has a good conscience; he whom a bad conscience accuses loses hope and expects nothing else but his own damnation.

Sinners fear all that could make them remember the other life; they fear retreat, which is so sweet for good

---

[38] See St. Augustine, *On Christian Doctrine*. I.40.44 (PL 34:36).

people; if they divert themselves, it is like those unfortunate ones who are condemned to death and who try to divert their thought from this by eating and drinking with their friends.

The sicknesses of the soul make, with regard to a Christian, the same effect upon the pleasures of life as the infirmities of the body: a sick man tastes nothing, the most exquisite foods are insipid, he finds the most delicious wines bitter, while a man who has health eats dry bread with a greater pleasure and quenches his thirst with pure water with delight.

What a misfortune to be unable to dwell one moment with oneself! These people hold solitude in horror. They incessantly need new pleasures; they who believe themselves happy by means of this are as simple as those who imagine that a woman who always smells of amber and musk is very healthy. These odors are often the remedies against the reek of a cancer or of a ruined lung, to which *remedies* she is obliged to have recourse in order to not smell this corruption, and in order to not pester others with it; so those persons who pass from pleasure to pleasure do so in order to charm the demon that torments them, even more, in order to hold off the feeling of their evils; these are perfumes in order to stop them from being suffocated by the reeking vapors which the dung of their conscience continually exhales.

Conscience in good people is a friend who renders pleasures more sensible and goods sweeter. Above all, it is a great help in adversities. It is for such a time that it is said, *Quid mihi est in cælo, et a te quid volui super terram [What is mine in heaven, and, except for You, what do I want upon earth]* (Ps 73:25)? It is at that time that God Himself tells us, through this voice: "What are you troubling yourself about? It is I Who brought this blow upon you, and you know well that I cannot hate you; you have lost your friend, your goods, your children: I can recompense you for all of this, I can take the place of all things for you." I remember Elkanah who consoles Anna in telling her, *Anna cur fles, et quare non comedis, et quamobrem affligitur cor tuum, numquid non ego melior tibi sum quam decem filii? [Anna, why are you weeping, and why aren't you eating, and why is your heart afflicted? Am I not better to you than ten sons?]* (1 Sm 1:8).

Conscience is a judge; some refuse to obey this judge; others corrupt this judge; others make it die.

As voice was given man in order to be the interpreter of his sentiments and of his desires, so it is through conscience that God teaches us that He judges each thing and what He expects from each of us. This divine voice forms diverse interior words in order to express the diverse lessons and the diverse orders which it has pleased God to give His creature; it is the bond of the commerce which the Lord greatly wants to have with us, and the most ordinary organ which serves Him in touching our hearts and in opening His to us.

One never despises with impunity the words which God has told us at the bottom of our soul, for beyond the harm we cause ourselves in rejecting the lights and the counsels of so luminous a wisdom, God never fails to avenge Himself; sometimes He pursues us in threatening us and in reproaching us for our ingratitude, and sometimes He draws away from us and keeps a silence towards us even more redoubtable than His reproaches. He punishes some by not ceasing to trouble them through bitter and piquant remorses, and some others by letting them enjoy a baneful repose in the midst of the greatest perils. Some find in Him an irritated and furious friend who gives them no respite, others, a cold and rejected friend who abandons them to their bad conduct and who takes no further part in what touches them.

Nothing makes one better see the burning desire God has had to guide men to sovereign felicity than the conscience that He has given them in order to serve them as a guide. Nothing so luminous for discerning good and evil, nothing so faithful for showing it to us, nothing so pressing for bringing us to embrace the one and flee the other, but if this conscience is an effect of His love, it is also one of His zeal for justice; for this same conscience, which is so careful in turning us away from evil, is also extremely severe in punishing us for it. Scarcely have we conceived the will to offend God when it begins to tear into us, to give us no more relief; from this come those emotions, that trembling, that confusion of spirit, those palpitations that a man feels who prepares himself to perform a crime, or who commits one.

From the time that one commits a crime, the conscience, which had counseled it otherwise at first, begins to strongly condemn it, to cry out against the malice of the hardened one, and to demand justice for the violence that one does to it, to take vengeance itself, but it is much worse when the crime is finished, for at that time, the pleasure having ceased, the passion having cooled, the souls remains prey to the sorrow and to the reproaches of the conscience; passion made it swallow poison without regarding it, lust watered it down with some sweetnesses, which disguised it in the mouth, but once it is in the entrails, it causes horrible pains. What a torture to hear that interior voice which cries out, which threatens, which takes pleasure in pressing, in renewing, at each moment, the cruel wound that sin caused in the soul!

One of the most awful wounds with which Moses struck Egypt was that number of frogs with which he filled it in a moment (Ex 8:1–15); those villainous animals slid about everywhere, even in Pharaoh's palace, even in his bed; they came to sully, with their infected drool, both his precious furniture and the very foods of his table, and they did not cease to interrupt his repose with their horrible croaks. This is an image of the war that a wicked Christian suffers due to his own crimes; they present themselves to him at all times, in all places, and always under a hideous form; they spare neither the hours of his affairs nor those of his pleasures; they ruin everything, they poison his most exquisite ragouts, they mix their frightening cries in with the most harmonious concerts, they trouble sleep and the most agreeable conversations. This is why Epicurus, the most voluptuous of all men, always excluded crime from his brutal felicity, although he would have composed it completely out of earthly and sensible pleasures.[39]

An ancient said that although crimes did not always come to the knowledge of men, although the gods themselves had promised him impunity for them, he would not be able to resolve himself to commit them; crime is itself so great a torture for he who commits it that it surpasses all the sufferings that the body can suffer in this life. This is why criminals have sometimes had recourse to human justice in order to deliver themselves, through death, from the reproaches of their conscience, preferring breaking wheels and gibbets, with all the ignominy which is attached to these kinds of torments, to the secret pains that their sins made

---

[39] In Epicurus's *Principal Doctrines*, he speaks of "natural justice," which is "a compact resulting from expediency by which men seek to prevent one man from injuring others and to protect him from being injured by them" (XXXI). He denies any idea of "justice in the abstract" (XXXII); he even claims that "injustice is not evil in itself" (XXXIV). This "compact" of natural justice between men is only kept due to fear of punishment for transgressing it (XXXIV–XXXV). Crime is excluded not out of any natural love for other men, but simply out of a fear of being punished by them. See Epicurus, *Letters, Principal Doctrines, and Vatican Sayings*, tr. Russel M. Geer (Indianapolis, IN: The Bobbs-Merrill Company, Inc., 1964), 63–64.

them suffer; there are some *pains* almost like those pains which conscience causes, like the sufferings that a stone or a toothache causes; nothing makes me better understand how sharp these sufferings are than seeing people who cut themselves, who rip out their teeth to solace themselves; what they suffer has to be very bitter, since they would rather attain healing by so cruel a martyrdom. But what ought one to think about the evils which an unfortunate man, whom his own crime pursues, endures, since he has recourse to dungeons, to a cruel and shameful death, in order to cure it? What such great charms does sin thus have that one would rather, for a moment of pleasure, expose oneself to this mortal fear, to these reproaches, to this confusion?

The silence of the conscience is to be feared even more after it has either spoken or even uselessly cried out for so long a time; it sometimes happens through an—indeed terrible, but nevertheless just—judgment that the conscience goes silent forever and leaves us in a mortal drowsiness, that is to say, that God retires His graces; in that state, all is silent, even the object which touches the sinner, even the discourse that rattles him, even the accident capable of terrifying him. At the death of Jesus Christ, all of nature spoke, all the wounds of the Son of God; these voices were spread by the good thief, by the torturers, by the dead, by the rocks; only the wicked thief, in the silence of his conscience, was insensible to all, all these voices were mute for him: these are the cursed trees like the fig (Mt 21:1–22); the sun, the dew, all was useless for him.

It is to be like the damned to fall into this state, which is, with regard to hell, what purgatory is with regard to paradise. His state cannot be eternal, and he cannot leave it except by passing into an eternity of pains. Thus, when the tare was noticed by the master of the field, he destined it for the fire, though it was not uprooted until the time of the harvest (Mt 13:30); God could make us die and toss us into hell after the last disdained grace; He is content with condemning us, He suspends the execution of His ruling, He leaves for us, still, some years of life, perhaps in order to pay, through this temporal recompense, for some good action we once did.

Saint Augustine says that God treats them easily, these insensible ones and these ones obstinate to the occasions for fall and for scandal, which every day drag them into new crimes. "I know well," says this saint, "that, when the will is carried towards evil, this is because it wills it, but there are certain causes, certain conjunctures, which draw the will on, and which engage it in this evil to which it is borne; now, it is God Who, through a very wise and very just providence, disposes these causes, it is God Who brings these baneful occasions to birth; He does not intend for them to bring *the will* to evil, and, thus, He does nothing against His sanctity, but He is not ignorant that they will bring it to this, and He exercises a terrifying justice upon these obstinate ones."[40] And this occurs often and to many. Of two kings, Saul abandoned; of two apostles, Judas hardened; of two thieves, one is insensible. And yet, to hear that man talk, he who has already suffocated all the remorse of his conscience, one would say that he has all the graces of heaven at his disposal, he hardily puts off till death all that one would beg him to do for his salvation. O vain and useless death, resource of the reproved, how long will the sinner regard you as an asylum against the wrath of his judge? You whom this same judge has destined to make the severity of His

---

[40] In *Retractions*, I.XV.3, Augustine emphasizes the necessity of the will in sin, even in unwitting sin: "Therefore, because he willed, he did it, even if he did not sin because he willed it, not knowing that what he did was sin; thus such a sin cannot be without the will, but by the will to act, not by the will to sin; yet this act was sin, for that was done which ought not to be done" (PL 32:609). I am not sure, though, where he discusses God leading the wicked into temptation in this way.

judgments shine over him. Even more, death itself—all frightful, all terrible as it is—will not touch him at all; in that moment, one will see a brutal assurance in him, which will make all those who assist him shiver with horror; he will die full of knowledge, he will see, he will understand, he will speak unto his last breath, and one will never hear him pronounce a word which marks his repentance; he is completely surrounded by religious, by priests, by Christian and zealous relatives, in the midst of the Sacraments and the prayers of the Church; and, notwithstanding all these aids, one sees him without repentance and without feeling, one will show him the crucifix, he will ask if it is made of silver, if it cost very much; the confessor will speak to him of hell, he will respond to him with a dart of mockery; his children will beseech him with tears to set his conscience in order, and he, as his full response, will recommend them to avenge him, as soon as possible, over an enemy whose throat death does not permit him to slit with his own hands. What a death! Is it possible that a Christian could envisage a miserable eternity so close, and be so little moved!

On Confession

It is a great disdaining of God to know that one is in His disgrace, His mortal enemy, that He is, however, disposed to receive us, and to not hasten to go ask pardon from Him, and to defer it for whole months; I am not unaware that it is easy to fall into sin, the penchant being so great, the passion sometimes so ardent, but when one has returned to his cold sense, to remain in this state—an injured man does not feel his wound in the heat of battle, but afterwards, he takes pleasure in seeing his blood run, so that he could sleep without having put on any clothes, so astonishing is it.

I am not as astonished at those who fear confession through not wanting to be corrected regarding their sins as at those who dread it for fear of discovering them: proof that it is a temptation is that one sees this dread in people who are in no way known by the confessor and who will never be known by him. What does this confessor hear in this confession except that there is someone in the village who has committed a fault?

You do no more harm to yourselves than if you had told it to a statue. The more the confessor recognizes you, the more he esteems you; the more pain there is, the more he will esteem that confidence that you have in him, and know that you have willingly chosen him to confide in him the worldly thing that it is most important for you to keep hidden. The more grievous the sin, the more the confessor recognizes you, the more merit there is, and consequently, the more the confessor will esteem you, if he is reasonable, if he has sentiments conformed to those of God and the angels, who see your humility with admiration, with joy. What extravagance in the confessor if he condemns you in his heart while God absolves you and heaps you with His graces! If he is not Christian, if he is mad, he will have these feelings, but if he is reasonable, if he has faith, he will admire you, he will praise God, he will weep with joy, he himself will overflow.

Perhaps you have done nothing so heroic in your life as this avowal of your sin, and you fear lest this disparage you in the spirit of a man who has a reason for humbling himself in seeing so great a virtue, who praises God effectively, who admires the force of His grace, who blesses His lovable providence, which permits falls in His elect in order to give them the occasion to raise themselves up to uncommon virtues, who weeps with joy and consolation, while you blush with shame, but you will forget all this if you fear God, if you love Him: you profit from your repugnance. The Master of sentences says that one will not speak, in the judgment, about sins for which one has done penance;[41] indeed, Saint Paul says, *Si nosmetipsos dijudicaremus, non utique judicaremur [If we have judged ourselves, certainly we shall not be judged]* (1 Cor 11:31).

It is strange that, of all the resolutions that men form, there is none that one fails to keep more than that of not offending God. A mark that one does not have a true sorrow over having offended God, that one does not repent over it, is that one does not fear this repentance. There is nothing as cruel as a true repentance; there is no man so vindicative that he will not believe himself well avenged when he makes his enemy do penance for the outrage he has committed against him.

This repentance is something so afflicting that it is insupportable; one must have force of spirit to bear it;

---

[41] Peter Lombard's *Book of Sentences* mentions multiple times that it is unjust to punish the same sin twice, and God is just: if a sin is truly forgiven in this life—and contrition and satisfaction are necessary for forgiveness—God will not punish that sin again in the final judgment. See Peter Lombard, *Book of Sentences*, IV.XV.1–2 (PL 192:872–873) and IV.XXII.1 (PL 192:897–898).

it has brought persons to despair; one more easily bears everything else: that is why it takes the place of our Judge of eternal pains; thus one calls it attrition, contrition, which not only injures the heart, it shatters it. And yet, everyday, with the intention of doing penance, I see that one offends God. I will confess, I believe it; if this were the only thing to do, I understand how it is that one would voluntarily expose oneself to all the confusion of confession in order to take a pleasure, but it is necessary to repent, so I will do penance; how will you repent? As you have done unto this hour. You will repent: this is not true; if you believed this well, you would not commit sin. You will repent: this is a reason to not do it, and if I had to turn you away from doing some action, I am sure that I would reach that goal if I could persuade you that you would someday have to repent for having done it. I know well that we deceive ourselves, but I do not know if God lets Himself be so deceived and if our error will save us.

It is necessary to ask God for this repentance; reflect if you have it, or if you don't have it. Consider what you do. Where are you going, miserable, hard-hearted, bad Christian, ingrate, insensible one? What will you do, irritate God even at the tribunal of His grace, insult Him, soil yourself with His Blood instead of purifying yourself, cause a shipwreck at port? You haven't committed enough crime, nor received enough graces: it's little enough to return a thousand times to ask for the same grace. This is why I go to it as coldly as the first time. Hell, paradise, the majesty of a God, all this could touch a man, but such a rock as I am, this is not yet sufficient.

Can one be assured that one is in grace after a well-made confession? One ought not doubt this; there are even Doctors who have taught that one could make an act of faith, just the same as one makes regarding the real presence of Jesus Christ in the Host, which the priest has consecrated.[42] But how will one know

---

[42] Ravier notes that this is an extreme view, and one that La Colombière himself backs away from in his *Sermon 73*, "On Christian Humility": "I know that there are Theologians who believe that one can be assured of having received pardon for one's faults with a Theological *certitude*, that is to say, the greatest certitude one can have in this world, after that of Faith; there are even those who have proposed that, after a reasonable penitence, one could believe that one has received remission, just as firmly as one believes that Jesus Christ is in the Host, over which one has pronounced the sacramental words. But, without stopping to explain these opinions, which, however, have a great need of being explained, it is a catholic truth that one cannot, on this point, have a certitude which excludes every kind of doubt, and, consequently, which hinders us from trembling." See Claude La Colombière, *Sermons prechez devant son altesse roïale madame la Duchesse d'Yorck* (Lyon: Anisson, Posuel, & Rigaud, 1684), IV:205–206.

that one has made a good confession? If, afterwards, a Christian lives far from occasions *of sin*, if he falls again no more. *Nunc vere scio quia misit Dominus Angelum suum, et eripuit me de manu Herodis et de omni expectatione plebis Iudæorum [Now I truly know that the Lord sent His Angel and snatched me from the hand of Herod and from all the expectation of the people of the Jews]* (Acts 12:11). Already the chains had fallen from his hands; he had passed the two guards' bodies, though he still believed he was dreaming, but when he had seen the iron gate open by itself, and when he was all alone on the road which led to Jerusalem, then he doubts no longer. *Nunc scio vere quia, etc.*

There is no fall which is repaired by tears except that which sin causes in us. So there is none but this which merits to be wept for, and yet one weeps for all the others, and one is in no way sensible to this one. Why is it that that little child who has lost its father does not stop laughing and enjoying himself? It is because he does not recognize the loss he has suffered; if he ever has reason, he will weep over it a thousand times. You have difficulty weeping over your sins, another has difficulty consoling himself; where does this come from, a lack of knowledge? Is it that I am not instructed in the reasons for contrition? You know them all, but you have not penetrated even one, and thus, it is your fault. You still love sin; you do not love God.

Many Doctors have believed that an Act of Contrition made in a moment does not suffice to efface sin, but it is certain that one moment of time does not suffice to excite contrition in a heart, except in the saints.[43]

If all confessions were good, there would be no more disorder; many accuse themselves of having enjoyed themselves too much: who will enjoy themselves less? For having not fasted last Lent, they are well resolved in their heart to do as much this Lent. Are you well resolved to be less greedy for gain, to vanquish

---

[43] Ravier (335–336, n. 2) gives a succinct background for the issue here: "We find ourselves, in truth, before the opinion, traditional in the Church until the Middle Ages, which incorporated the time of satisfaction into Penance, before considering that the sinner was pardoned. The base text is that of Fulgentius of Ruspe, who formulates the triple condition of pardon: 'Faith, work, time' (*On the Remission of Sins* I.5, PL 65:531B). This opinion was so well admitted that, for a long time, the possibility of a deathbed pardon, or a 'sudden repentance' was doubted (Augustine, *Sermon* 393, PL 39:1714; Faustus of Riez, *Sermon* 255, PL 39:2216; Cesarius, *Sermon* 256, PL 39:2217–2218). One had to wait for Abelard in order to formulate the possibility of an instantaneous pardon: *Dialogue Between a Philosopher, a Jew, and a Christian*, PL 178:1634. Even the possibility of a sudden contrition was placed in doubt. Thus Hugh of Saint-Victory, *On the Sacraments*, Book II, Part 14, Ch. 12, PL 176:547A–C."

that antipathy you have towards your neighbor; you avenged yourself: do you really have a very great sorrow over this? You would be in despair if you had not done it; if you had to do it again, you would do it, and in order to make you see that this sin pleases you, it is so that you will boast of it at every encounter, and if one gives you a similar occasion, you will not fail to take a similar vengeance. At the bottom, it is only a grimace, as at the death of great men; all the world puts on mourning and comes to pay compliments of condolence; the majority take delight in this.

On Deferred Repentance

You defer your repenting, doing penance: will you do more at the hour of death than the foolish virgins? They ask for aid, they run to do good works, they return with trimmed lamps, they knock, they cry out, and nevertheless, one does not open to them (Mt 25:8–12). If I propose to you, today, to make a review, to set all things in order from today henceforth, as if you were to die, to make your testament, your general confession, to examine all the actions, all the confessions of your life, to see, a little bit, what you possess, what you owe, your detractions, your scandals, etc. You would tell me that this is not an affair for a single day, that you would need to make a retreat for this, to regulate the affairs that remain in your hand, so that nothing would trouble your spirit; if you had the least fever, the least headache, you would tell me that you need to wait for health, that, in the state you're in, you are capable of nothing, and at the hour of death, it will be much worse; there will still be more to do, for this increases every day.

It is no longer the time to do penance at the end; this is the time which justice has reserved to recompense or to punish. Either God is mocked, or this is true: you laughed at His threats, He will laugh at your tears. His providence must act in this way. This is why a good man dying makes you see, as it were, an image of paradise, or at the least, of purgatory, and the wicked *man dying*, of hell. Has God not made hell in order to oblige us to die well? He made it to oblige us to live well, to keep us within our duty, to prevent the disorders that license and the passions would cause in the world, but what will it serve for if I can live as if there were no hell and, nevertheless, secure myself at death by saying *peccavi [I have sinned]*?

Subito morientur, et in media nocte turbabuntur populi et pertransibunt [Suddenly, they will die, and, in the middle of the night, people will be shaken and will pass away] (Job 34:20). *Turbabuntur [They will be shaken]*: here is their penitence, and so it will be that they will die in this trouble and in this confusion. The good death is the last grace, which one can merit no more than the first; God imitates the great painters in this, they who always place the first and last strokes on their paintings; they abandon all that is between the design and the completion to the good painters who labor under them, but as they never fail to make a sketch for them, since the beauty of the design and the proportion of the parts depends on this, so they reserve the last touch for themselves. No austerity, no virtue, no action, however heroic it could be, can impose on God an obligation of justice to give you death in grace. But even that man who has lived sixty years in the rigors of penance, who trembles at the sight of death, that saint who has never lost his innocence, who, from his baptism, lived not a single moment outside of grace, is not assured of dying in it, and that young libertine who, from the age of reason, has never, perhaps, been without mortal sin, believes that God must grant him so distinguished a favor? Tell me, then, I pray you, what you have done to expect, with so much certitude, so extraordinary a grace: you are His enemy, you mocked Him a thousand times, you have lived in extreme disdain of His commandments, and you pretend that, as recompense, He will bestow upon you the greatest of all graces. If a Saint Paul promised it to himself, he would be a temerarious man; he can hope for it, but he ought to fear, and you, libertine, shameless one, you live without disquiet, as if God had revealed to you that you will die like a saint?

One would say that men are the arbiters of life and grace, and that they are assured of dying the kind of death that will please them, and to have, at that time, the grace that is necessary for them. Now, look at what their assurance is founded upon. He who is the arbiter of these two choices is their mortal enemy: what makes it seems like He would grant them to them? He has even protested that He will refuse them to them, and thus it is infallible that He will not grant them; they base themselves upon a God Whom they have irritated, upon a God Who declared Himself for the contrary. I am not astonished that the favorite of a prince commits crimes with the hope of impunity, and that he is promised grace—which will be necessary for him—by his master, but a rebel, a traitor, a man hated unto death, etc.

Nothing persuades me more strongly that those who defer their repentance are in error than the experience one has that old people do not convert. It is true that great evils are done from the age of twenty years until thirty, but it is necessary to avow that great conversions still happen then; one sees few thereafter. I call "conversion" the change that one makes from a vain or sensual or libertine life to a humble, mortified, regulated life.

In youth, vices are in the mouth, in the eyes, in the flesh that revolts and that one does not repress, in the blood that beats, but in the old, these same vices are in the bones; they sin through the memory of the past, through useless desires, but yet criminals of the present. Old age takes necessary forces away from the spirit and body; it no longer acts except by habit; very far from suffocating the vices and the habits one has contracted, it brings in new ones; it is despondent, attached to its senses, damaged, defiant, timid; while one does not bear the vices of youth in old age, one is hindered enough from combating those one finds there. It is necessary to prevent, though youth's combats, the weaknesses of the last age, very far from sending the habits contracted in the flower of age there to be undone.

When one does in old age what one did not do *before*, this is not virtue, for what force, what victory, to triumph over a vanquished, defeated, dead enemy? To be abstinent when you no longer have taste, chaste when the blood is frozen in the veins, and when one forms a horror for all the world. It is as if a disgusted invalid wanted to make a merit of his abstinence, or a man full of wine and food, of the fact that he eats no more. One wants to give oneself to God in an age when we wouldn't want to receive a man into our service, and when one is often undone by those who have served us all their life. Those people who defer their repentance to old age are debtors who, having enough silver to pay their debts, dissipate it and coldly defer their creditors until the time when they have nothing to acquit themselves with; does it seem that the creditors will wait until that time?

It is an extravagance to defer repentance, since it is uncertain that one will have the leisure to do it; it would be useless for God to goad us so strongly if nothing goaded in truth; why does He warn us to keep watch if there is nothing to fear? He does not tell us "put your accounts in order," but "render your accounts"; He does not say "prepare yourselves," but "be ready *to pay*." One cannot prepare oneself except through a continual repentance; it is the sole means of repairing sin, it is the unique means of repairing it; you want to relieve yourself, do penance; you want to fall no more, do penance; it will destroy the committed sin through sorrow and satisfaction in such a way that it is no longer habitually there, destroy it through distancing from relapses in such a way that it is no longer actually there; if it were only necessary to tell one's faults and confess, the affair would soon be done; above all, today, one is not content to avow them, one publishes them, one glories in them. The penitent is the man in wrath against himself. Judge for yourself if there are many penitents.

The justice of God is better satisfied—or, to say it better, one would satisfy the justice of God better—through small pains than through great tortures, through a short penance than through an eternal repenting, through a sorrow mixed with joy than through a wholly pure sorrow, like that of hell. The reason: penance is voluntary, and consequently, spirit, liberty, bends beneath the justice of God instead of, in hell, the will being eternally in rebellion; the former destroys sin, the great enemy of God; it subsists in hell; the other does not appease His wrath, this one changes it into love.

Sin alone merits our tears; tears efface sin, and sin sweetens tears; tears poured out for sin efface it and become sweet. They are useless and bitter when one pours them out for another reason. *Cinerem tanquam panem manducabam, et potum meum cum fletu miscebam [Ash I eat like bread, and my drink I mix with weeping]* (Ps 102:9). I would find the same taste in repentance as in the most favored foods.

We are, because of sin, like those persons who have ruined temperament and altered principles, who no longer live except through the cares of medicine; one cannot heal the source of the evil; it is more that one hinders the effects through continual remedies and through an uninterrupted regime. But if one ceases, for a moment, to give them these remedies, if they abandon the rules of the doctor, they will die a sudden death, the humors coming to overflow.

On Frequent Communion

If, before the coming of the Savior of the world into these ages of iron and rigor, when the Lord made Himself to be called the avenging God, the mighty God, the God of arms, when He did not speak except through the voice of thunder, when He demanded so respectful a worship, and when He punished, with such severity, the very little faults one committed against respect, if, I say, in that time, one had foreseen, with a little more clarity, what we have since seen, if the Israelites had well understood the sense of so many figures, of the sacrifice of Melchizedek (Gn 14:17–24), of the Manna (Ex 16), of the Bread of Gideon (Jgs 6:19–21), of that of Elijah (1 Kgs 17:6), of the Bread of the presence (Lv 24:5–9) and the others, if one had told them that this so terrible God would abase Himself unto our altars, that His love would bring Him to give Himself entirely to become our food, our daily bread, that He would descend between the hands of all priests, that He would let Himself be handled, carried, enclosed, exposed to eyes and outrages, etc., finally, eaten and enclosed in our stomachs, as often as it pleased us, would they have been able to believe it?

Something has happened which would have appeared even more incredible to them; would they have been able to believe that a God, abasing Himself in this way, giving Himself, lavishing Himself, one would refuse to receive Him? That so exquisite a food would not excite our appetite, that one would hold it in disgust, like the Manna (Nm 11:4–6), that one would be constrained to command that this Bread be eaten, and that one would command it under pain of death? Yet this has happened; there are Christians, and in great number, who are forced to eat this bread, etc.[44]

This pretended respect that those who distance themselves from Communion prescribe makes me recall the false modesty of Saint Peter, which brought him to refuse to have Jesus Christ wash his feet, which was condemned in so strong a manner, and which would have made him lost, without recourse, if he had

---

[44] A reference to the "Easter duty," the canonical requirement to receive Communion during the Paschal season; this is discussed again at the end of this chapter.

not changed his sentiment: *Nisi lavero tibi pedes non habebis partem mecum in* æternum *[Unless I wash your feet, you will not have a part with Me in eternity]* (Jn 13:8). In the measure that one is engaged in the world, one has more trouble Communing, so that one does not have to preach to the vicious to refrain from Communion; they do it enough themselves, and one does not see those souls, corrupted and plunged into disorder, being famished for this heavenly food.

All the spiritual Fathers agree that the best mark one could have of the solidity of a practice of devotion is the amendment of our mores and perseverance in the good. You tell me that there is some illusion in Communing so frequently, every eight days, for example;[45] that it would be better to do it more rarely, but who is it that you preach this new doctrine to? To me, who drew myself from disorder only by this way, after having tried all the others uselessly? While I frequented the Eucharist only rarely, I was plunged into bad habits, into imperfections which appeared insurmountable to me; I uprooted these old habits by multiplying my Communions, and you want me to believe that it

---

[45] Ravier notes that weekly Communion was a rarity in La Colombière's time; for recommending it, he was sometimes even accused of Jansenism (343, n. 2).

is the demon who brings me to this practice? Every time I interrupted this custom, I felt myself weaker, I knew that *my habits* had, the same day, fallen into their first deregulations; when I returned to it, I felt the fervor rekindle in my heart. I know, through my own experience and through that of a million persons, that all bad Christians agree with your counsel and, without delay, they distance themselves from the use of the sacraments by their own full will. I know that never has a fervent Christian grown lax without beginning by quitting the sacraments, except for those who, approaching it in bad faith, for human respect or for a kind of necessity, have preferred committing sacrileges to quitting their disorders, and you want me to believe that I deceive myself? If I saw that, in Communing every eight days, instead of being reformed, I did not stop feeling the same weakness, the same tendency into evil, the same indifference for mortal sin; at that time, I would believe, not that I ought to abstain from it, but rather bring better dispositions to it; at that time, I would believe, or, at least, I would have reason to understand, that my confessions lacked either sincerity or sorrow or resolution to amend myself. You are wicked; amend yourself, as soon as possible in order to

On Frequent Communion

Commune often; you are imperfect, Commune often in order to amend yourself.

The use of the Holy Sacrament is like friendship: it is preserved by frequent sight and conversation; without pain, one does without a person one has left without regret,[46] one even comes to forget him. Absence heals the most violent passions. But if it happens that I abuse Communion, that I draw no profit from it, that I do not amend myself: ought I not to quit Communion? No, but rather regulate your life and undo the vices that hinder you from profiting from it; the fault comes not from your Communing too often but from your Communing badly, and thus, the counsel that you ought to take at that time is not to absent yourself from Communion but from the vices that hinder its fruit.

Every nourishment is useless to you since you take it inopportunely, or since it is poorly seasoned; what counsel would you take on this occasion: to eat nothing at all or to regulate your repast and to do better at seasoning your foods? A remedy useful to all the world is useless to me by lack of some precautions which I neglected until this hour. Ah! Do continue to take the remedy but do it with the necessary precautions.

---

[46] The first edition erroneously has "one has left only with regret," but this is corrected in the second edition and later.

There is a man who eats well and who takes an excellent nourishment every day; however, because he sets himself at table after leaving too hard and too long a study, because he brings all his thoughts there, and because, even while eating, in his spirit, with focus, he keeps going over things that he read or meditated over before the repast, because, as soon as he has eaten, he returns to his study, and begins his labor again with an extraordinary contention of spirit, the spirits which ought to serve digestion, being called elsewhere by his intellectual functions, leave the stomach destitute of the aid they need, wherefore the foods are corrupted in him, so that he is full of bad humors, which alter his temperament and cause him a thousand sufferings. Despite assembling all the most skilled doctors, despite consulting all the academies, will there ever be found a single man who will order this sick man to take no more nourishment, to abstain from eating? "Let him be less apt to study," all will say with one voice, "let him quit it for a moment before the repast, let him forget all his books during the time he's eating, and before reopening them, let him give nature leisure to perform its functions and to digest what he has taken in." But one has already given him this counsel a hundred times uselessly. It is so much the worse for him that he does not follow it; he enjoys losing himself without support, but when one consults us about it a thousand times, one ought not to expect another response from us. "But if he does not eat, at least the food would not corrupt itself within his stomach"; it is true, but he would die of weakness; study would not hinder digestion, but it would soon exhaust the rest of his forces, and you would see him fall, in twenty-four hours, in a mortal languor; he would not die of indigestion, but of hunger; one would hinder that mass of bad humors that covers him, but you would dry out the radical wet[47] that makes him live. In a word, it would be foolish to take from him that by which he lives in order to deliver him from that which makes him sick;

---

[47] The traditional doctrine of the four humors (blood, phlegm, black bile, yellow bile) analyzed them under four characteristics: hot, cold, wet, and dry. Ravier gives a brief summary of the medicinal beliefs underlying this paragraph: "The *spirits* are light and subtle bodies, principles of life and of feelings. They are close kin to the *animal spirits* which are the vital fluid formed in the heart and in the brain, and transmitted through the body by the nerves. The *humors* are four in number (blood, phlegm, bile, and black bile), and their more or less perfect equilibrium gives rise to *temperament*. The *radical wet [humide radical]* is either the fluid, principle of life of organized beings, or the liquid which, being delivered to the diverse organic tissues via circulation, gives them appropriate consistency and flexibility" (345, n. 1).

he needs to eat, but he needs to do it with the necessary precautions. Return to the doctor a thousand times, he will never tell you anything else: "That sick man does not change his conduct: what do you want me to do?" If he is imprudent, if he is indiscreet, if he is obstinate and stubborn, the doctor has no remedy against those evils; if he has resolved to kill himself, he can either eat or not eat, he will die just as well in one way as the other, and even faster by eating nothing. This is a parable, Messieurs: apply it to those who always return to their first imperfections, who do not come to the Holy Table with the devotion that it needs; there is nothing so just nor which relates more exactly.

A man who Communes at Pascha, while being currently in mortal sin and in a wicked way of life, he sins, doubtless, but there is a Commandment of the Church which obliges him to Commune, but there is one of God, which forbids him to Commune in a bad state, but if he does not Commune, does he sin? Doubtless he sins, and very grievously, but it would be a sacrilege if he did it; he would not sin if he abstained from Communion for fear of committing a sacrilege, but he only abstains in order to not be obliged to renounce his wicked way of life, which is a diabolical reason. If he fears naught but sacrilege, does he not avoid it by departing from his sin?

God forbids you to Commune in mortal sin, at whatever time it be, but the Church orders you to quit your sin at Pascha in order to Commune, and this under the pain of a new mortal sin. To clarify this point, and to make you understand it, there are two Christians, one of whom is in a habit of adultery, or of blasphemy, and the other is in the state of grace. The first does not want to Commune, since he wants to continue his adulteries and his blasphemes; the other no longer wants to Commune due to negligence, due to laziness, due to a certain laxness, which renders him all numb and as if stupid, since he wants to have breakfast before leaving the house.[48] Who of the two sins more grievously in not Communing on the day of Pascha? Could one doubt that it is the first, and that the sin which he commits surpasses the other in malice, as much as adultery and blasphemy surpass a light intemperance of the mouth? Both mortally sin in disobeying the Church, but I say that the disobedience of the blasphemer is, without comparison, more criminal, just the same as a gentleman who refuses to go to the army in order to have the occasion of corrupting the wife of his sovereign renders himself more culpable

---

[48] The traditional fast before receiving Communion required the communicant to eat nothing that day before receiving Communion; today, the required fast is only for an hour before Communion.

than he who refuses to take up arms in order to make good cheer with his friends. There is a double sin in the blasphemer: the first of disobedience to the Church, the second of attachment to blasphemy and immodesty, but a formal attachment, and in such a way that, although he knows the obligation he has of leaving it, that the Church solicits him, warns him, goads him, threatens him with excommunication if he does not acquit himself of his duty, he prefers to disobey her, scandalize her, expose her to having a number of her children taken away from her, deprive himself of the good fortune of receiving his God within his breast, and of participating in the infinite treasures with which He would heap him during this visit, rather than to quit his deregulations, rather than to become a friend of God.

This reproach is stronger still against me than against you, since I do receive that adorable Body of my Savior, not only often, but every day. What! A priest, who makes Jesus Christ descend upon our altars every day, who touches Him, who distributes Him to the people, who himself Communes every day, an heir of the priesthood of Jesus Christ, the Mediator established between heaven and earth, after ten, twenty, thirty years of priesthood, after eight or ten thousand Communions, to still hold to the world through some bond, to still be less pure than the angels, to still not be more burning than the Seraphim, to still not be sanctified and even deified! A priest who nourishes himself, every day, on the bread of angels, who dips his tongue, every day, in the Blood of Jesus Christ, to use that same tongue for detraction and cajolery, to make it serve as an instrument for wrath and for vengeance, to nourish, in his heart, passions of hate, of pride, of avarice, to have criminal attachments, to be a man, to be, sometimes, worse than the beasts, to be a visible and incarnate demon! O God, O angels, O power, O character, O opprobrium, O shame of the Church, O scandal of Christianity!

On the Mass

The priest is naught but the minister of the Church, that is to say, of all those who are present at the Mass; the victim whom he immolates does not belong to him except insofar as he is a part of the Church; it is to the Church that Jesus Christ left it, it is the Church who offers it and, consequently, all those who hear the Mass. This is why hearing Mass and making profession of Christianity is all one; just as to sacrifice to idols was to be an idolater through the profession that one was found in the temple of the false Gods at the hour of sacrifice. But if a Christian had entered there at that same hour, while those poor blind men prostrated their faces against the ground in a prodigious silence, and if he had gone there to do what we see so often done in our churches—chatting, laughing, conversing while standing or sitting—this action would have passed for a manifest profanation and for an all-visible scorn of their false divinities.

God is more honored by a single Mass than He could be by all the other actions of both angels and men, however fervent and however heroic they could be, but who goes to Mass with the design to render God so extraordinary an honor? Who thinks with pleasure of the glory that He receives from this Sacrifice? Who rejoices to have the ability to so honor Him according to His merits and His grandeur? Who gives thanks to Jesus Christ for abolishing all the other sacrifices? He has left us a Host that God cannot fail to accept, a Host proportioned to the benefits we have received from Him and, for those who can ask Him, a Host capable of effacing all the sins of men. Yes, my God, when I pray, when I fast, when I give alms, I do it with defiance, perhaps (I say within myself), for I dishonor God more by my bad intentions, by the circumstances of my action, than I honor Him through my action. This repentance, far from effacing my crimes, perhaps itself has need of repentance. This almsgiving that I do in order to testify to my gratitude, it is, perhaps, an offense which I render for a thousand benefits. But when I say the Mass, or when I hear it, when I offer the Adorable sacrifice in the quality of a minister, or of a member of the Church, it is then—my God!—that, full of confidence and courage, I dare to defy all

On the Mass

of heaven, to do something that pleases You more; it is then that, without being frightened by the number nor by the enormity of my crimes, I dare to ask pardon from You, not even doubting that You will grant it to me in the most perfect manner that I would know how to hope for. However vast be my desires, however far be my hopes, I have no difficulty in asking from You all that is capable of fulfilling them. I ask You for graces and for great graces, and all sorts of graces for myself, for my benefactors, for all my friends, for my most mortal enemies, and, very far from blushing at my request, very far from being wary of obtaining so many things at the same time, I find that I ask little in comparison to what I offer. I believe I am doing harm to that living Host in asking infinitely less than it is worth; I fear nothing so much as not expecting, with a firm and constant assurance, both all that I have asked and something even grander, if it is possible, than all that I could ask. Ah! May it please God that we would well understand the value of the treasure that we have between our hands. Happy and a thousand times happy the nation of Christians if they know how to profit from their advantages. What source of all kinds of goods will you not find in this adorable Sacrifice, what graces, what favors, what temporal and spiritual riches for the body, for the spirit, for life, for eternity! But it is necessary to avow the truth: we do not even think of serving ourselves with our goods, we do not deign to even put our hand upon the treasure which Jesus Christ has left to us.

Indeed, what esteem do we hold towards the Mass, with what intentions do we come to it? What do we do when we are there? You come there by custom, through human respect: God forbid that it be for even more criminal reasons. You entertain yourself there with a thousand vain thoughts; you amuse yourself by considering the ornaments of the Church, or the persons who are sitting with you; you chatter with someone solicits you, or else one is yawning, one is bored, one doesn't know what to occupy oneself with. What, then! Have you never received any favor from the good God? Have you thanked Him for it as you must, with feeling, with tenderness? Take guard lest you, through lack of recognition, dry up the benefits of God towards you, and lest you turn them away from you. It is strange that we are surrounded, charged, and heaped with favors from the good God, that, from the first moment of our life until today, He has loved us, He has preserved us, He has carried us in His arms, and that we have never thanked Him for it as we ought.

To occupy yourself during Mass, go over these benefits: so many perils turned away, so many crimes concealed, so loving and so constant a Providence exercised over you, to procure for you baptism, a Christian education, a sure, honest, comfortable, advantageous establishment, to distance the objects, the occasions, the dangers in which you would have lost grace, innocence, life, goods, and honor, so sweet and so continual a hastening to draw you to Him, to win your heart, to make you a saint, and a hundred other things I don't know how to say. Detailing the graces you receive in a single day would be sufficient to occupy you throughout the whole Mass. Does all this not well merit to be remembered? After having gone over all these benefits in your spirit, say hardily to the Eternal Father, "Lord, this is what I have received from You, but see this Host, this Divine Body, this precious Blood, this adorable Sacrifice, this is what I render You for so many benefits; I cannot doubt that they are very well paid by so magnificent a present. But what can I render You, my adorable Master! You Who have granted me to so freely recognize the benefits of Your Father by which to expiate all my sins."

You don't know what to do at Mass; have you never offended God? Do you not offend Him every day and every hour of the day? During Mass, go over all the faults you have committed since the Mass of the preceding day, etc. Ask Him for pardon, but do you have need of nothing? You complain every day about your relatives, about your friends, about your children, about your wives. Ask God that He might render that enemy more reasonable, that daughter more modest, that husband less boorish, that wife less disgruntled, and in order to obtain all these graces, offer Him Jesus Christ in sacrifice. You have indocile, libertine, debauched children; they make you dry up with sorrow; they have no piety towards God, no respect for their mother, nor obedience to you: every day they give you a thousand displeasures, they make you spend your life in tears and in sorrow. Perhaps, although it is your fault, you have been too indulgent towards them, you have not watched over their conduct from the beginning, you have entirely neglected their education, you have asked God for them with too much eagerness, but that's past, the evil is done: it is necessary to bring the remedy. Ask God that He would reform your work, that He would repair what you have ruined, that He would change the heart of this son, and, finally, so that He cannot refuse you this grace, offer Him the unbloody Victim Who is immolated upon the altar; He won't be able to refuse you. You are wrathful, impatient, carried away, you cannot undo your thousand wicked habits which tyrannize you; you see well that, if you die here, you are damned; ask God that He might deliver you from this.

Your sins, your relapses, your weakness cause you pain; you well desire to correct them, to surmount this repugnance, this tepidity, to break this little attachment, which is the only thing that holds you to earth; there is a year, there are ten, when you fight against an imagination, against an atom, against I know not what, which hinders you from being all God's and from enjoying that peace which accompanies a completely free, completely pure heart. Ah, my God! Are they heretics or barbarians who hold these discourses with me? But what? A Christian? Can he desire something in vain? Have you asked these things from God? How often have you offered Masses to God in order to obtain them? Do you want me to believe that a God presented as the price of these graces is incapable of obtaining them? God has refused them to you, to you, that might be, but have you asked them through Jesus Christ, have you offered Him, as the price of these graces, the blood of a God, the life of a God, the Victim you have in your hands; do you hear Mass every day to obtain them?

"Without the Sacrifice of the Mass," says a Doctor, "the world would have already been sunk a thousand times; it is this which stops the arm of God, irritated by so many crimes."[49] This is why the demon tries to take it away from us by means of heretics, since he sees well that we would all perish without this breaker, which is opposed to the vengeance of God. So the prophet Daniel predicted that the antichrist would abolish it at the end of times: *Et robur datum est contra juge sacrificium propter peccata [And strength was given* him *against the continual sacrifice because of sins]* (Dn 8:12). Saint Hippolytus Martyr, reported by St. Jerome, describing what will occur in those last times, says that the Churches will be in an extreme decay since sacrifice will not be made there. Nowhere will one have either the Body or the Blood of Jesus Christ; the Mass will be abolished, and so it will be until the world ends and

---

[49] The closest quote I have found is attributed to St. Leonard of Port Maurice (1676–1751); however, he was born only a few years before La Colombière died, so he cannot be the latter's source. See Stefano M. Manelli, *Jesus Our Eucharistic Love* (New Bedford, MA: Academy of the Immaculate, 1996), 15: "I believe that if there were no Mass, the world would by now have sunk into the abyss under the weight of its wickedness. The Mass is the powerful support that sustains it." Ravier was also unable to find a source for this quote (353, n. 1).

until it is judged.[50] But while this innocent Lamb is immolated upon our altars, this cannot occur.

It is strange that the Lord cannot fill His house except by using violence and forcing us, in some way, to enter it. For, indeed, He needed express commandments in order to oblige the faithful to come into the churches to hear Mass there, as if the fruits that we draw from this divine sacrifice were not sufficient to draw us there. But one does not know these ineffable fruits; this ignorance is one of the things that we have most cause to deplore in Christianity. What a misfortune that we have an immense and inexhaustible treasure in our midst and that, by not recognizing it, we live in indigence! That we have, in our power, a remedy for all sorts of evils,

---

[50] St. Jerome quotes St. Hippolytus as saying that "For another three years, under the Antichrist, host and sacrifice will be lacking" (*Commentary on Daniel*; PL 25:548A). A more detailed account is found in a work falsely ascribed to St. Hippolytus; see Pseudo-Hippolytus, *On the End of the World*, §34: "Then the Churches too will lament a great lament, for they shall complete no offering nor incense nor God-worthy worship; but the holy places of the Churches will be like a fruit-watcher's hut, and the precious Body and Blood of Jesus will not be shown forth in those days; liturgy will be extinguished, psalmody will cease, reading of the Scriptures will not be heard. But there will be darkness for men, and lamentation upon lamentation, and woes upon woes" (PG 10:936D–937A).

a tree of life that could communicate to us not only health but even immortality, and that, nevertheless, we are heaped with infirmities, we live a languishing life, we every day die the most baneful of all deaths! The Mass is that universal remedy, that tree of life, that rich treasure; it belongs to each of us; we only have to reach out our hand and enrich ourselves in the easiest way in the world, and yet I perceive, and I perceive with extreme regret, that one despises this treasure, that one does not deign to profit from it. There is the appearance that the great number of Masses that are celebrated every day and in all places in the church is the reason some make such little use of this Mystery, and that, thus, it happens that the liberality of our God, which ought to increase our gratitude, has a completely contrary effect and brings us to ingratitude.

There is nothing so poor as man; he has nothing which is his, and very far from being able to acquit himself of what he owes, he lacks everything necessary, and he is constrained to contract new debts every day in order to subsist. We owe much, and we have nothing; we owe, to the grandeur of God, an homage, and an homage in such a way that it would respond to that infinite grandeur. We owe His goodness all that we have, all that we are, and to His justice, the satisfaction of our crimes, which are nearly infinite in number, and which are absolutely infinite in their malice. Beyond this, we are in an extreme indigence of all kinds of goods; we have need of extraordinary aid in order to live, to live comfortably, to live tranquilly, to live Christianly, finally, to die holily, and to pass from this life to a better one. Where to acquire what would acquit so many debts, where to furnish enough needs? The Mass furnishes us, in abundance, what would acquit all those debts and what would satisfy all those needs.

When Jesus Christ died, He made satisfaction for our sins, but this satisfaction did not have its effect at that time, for we were not yet in the world; it is applied to us every day through the renewal of His death that is made at the altar. When you are at Mass, there is done for you what was done upon Calvary for those who were present if you will to profit from it.

On Calvary, if you had been there, would He have been able to refuse you pardon? Here, it is the same thing with regard to effect. But what happens in regards to this intention, what happens if a criminal, if a sick man, in the state of a penitent, if Jesus Christ finds him there? There is often none but him; at the cross, there were naught but a few people who profited from it; the same here: if we go to it in this spirit, it would avail us more than all penances, we would expiate all our sins—I can't believe that there could be a purgatory for us. But, alas! I fear, on the contrary, that there is an occasion for a long and rigorous purgatory for us because of our tepidity, because of the manner in which we comport ourselves. What misfortune, to not content ourselves with losing our goods, but even to turn the most salutary remedies into poison for ourselves!

We ought to give thanks to God for all the goods we have received. These goods are infinite, if we have a bit of heart, a bit of humanity; ingratitude ought to be very odious to us. But beyond the infamy attached to this vice, it is infinitely pernicious to us with regard to God; it dries up all the sources of graces. This is why Jesus Christ, seeing that we have nothing with which we might testify to God about our gratitude, He gave Himself to us, and gives Himself to us every day so that, receiving new benefits every day, we could worthily thank God every day, and this thanksgiving is not a vain compliment; it is an effective recognition, greater than if you gave Him all the empires of the world, but who thinks of it?

Jesus Christ, at the Mass, places Himself in our hands like a coin of infinite price, in order to buy from God all that we could desire from Him, however precious be the good we request. Jesus Christ makes Himself, in the sacrifice of the Mass, not only our intercessor to His Father, in order, through His merits, to ask for all that is necessary to us, all that we hope for, but He offers there His Blood and His Life, as if in payment for what we request. What could you desire that is so grand that it is above what you present to receive it? Why is it, then, that the whole world complains, some of their temporal miseries, some of their spiritual faults? Why is it that the passions tyrannize us, that bad habits hold us as if enchained, that one is importuned by impure thoughts, the other by temptations against the Faith, that wrath and impatience plunge some, every day, into regrettable rages, for which they repent a moment later, that sorrow heaps upon others, and that it brings them even to despair? Why is it that this woman cannot sweeten her husband, nor draw him back from debauchery, that she cannot have peace, although she desires it, that this father sees, with regret, his children take a bad route? One wants to amend, correct, and reform others, and yet he does none of this for himself? It seems to me that I see an avaricious man who lacks everything, although he does not lack gold and silver. Have you asked for this at Mass? How many times have you heard it for this intention? Will you persuade me that God, for so great a price, has refused you so little a thing? That He has valued the Blood, the Life of His Son, so little that He did not believe it was worth this grace, this virtue, this temporal or spiritual good that you hope for, either for you or for another? No, I will never believe this, and I am sure that you yourself will not believe it: what is it, then? It is that you neglect to assist at Mass and to present to God, during this precious time of salvation and of acceptance—you fail, I say, to present your miseries to God at that time, and to request from Him the graces that you hope for.

On Irreverence
in Churches

To render some place Holy which could be so, it suffices that it be destined to honor God; from the moment when it is solemnly consecrated to this use, it becomes venerable to the angels, terrible to the demons, and it would be very just for the Majesty of God, with which it is filled, from that time, in a special way, to also render it formidable to all men.

All the sanctity which the birth of the Son of God communicates to the stable of Bethlehem, all that His Blood communicates to Calvary, and His dead Body to the sepulcher, all of it is found in the churches of Christians, and as soon as I enter them, as soon as I approach the altars, I do not feel myself penetrated by that holy fright with which one is seized when approaching holier places; if I am not touched by the same sentiments, which make such sweet tears run from the eyes of those who have the good fortune to see the Créche in which

Jesus was born, if I do not feel those transports of love and of joy which make some people expire in adoring the mountain where God Himself was crucified, or in kissing the footsteps that He left imprinted when ascending to heaven, it is only through a lack of faith or a lack of attention.

It is in our churches, in that tabernacle, that the Body of the Savior reposes; it was in the womb of Mary for only nine months, only forty days in the stable, only three hours upon the cross, only three days in the sepulcher, and it is always in our churches; this is why they are never empty of angels, of archangels, of Seraphim, who do not cease to adore it with respects and humiliations, which would strangely confound us if we could perceive them.

Our churches, if one can speak in this way, are like an annex to paradise; the Creator is adored there, the resurrected Savior finds a Body and a Soul there, the heavenly spirits make their sojourn there, and there they enjoy the same happiness that one tastes above the firmament. It is this adorable place that our libertines choose for exercising coquetry, for producing their pride, for flaunting their vanity and their insolence. "If we had a bit of Faith," Saint Chrysostom remarks, "would we dare to appear there after having committed

On Irreverence in Churches

in secret the crimes which we come there to commit in the face of heaven and earth?"[51]

One would be strangely shocked if one saw a Christian laugh upon Calvary and cajole in the same place where the Savior was crucified, but how much more horrible would it be if this were done at the time when He was currently dying there!

What do you go to Church to do, bad Catholic? Do you go to render your respects to God and to humbly confess that you are naught but a vile slave, but a bit of dust, that you are nothing in His presence? One would say, on the contrary, upon seeing the care that you took in adorning yourself, one would say, upon seeing the air with which you enter that place, that you are the divinity of the Temple, that you aim to snatch God's adorers away from Him and to draw their worship, as well as their regards, to yourself. Is it to recognize your indigence, to ask from some grace from Him, that you come there? If you have a debt to demand from a farmer, would you do it with more pomp? Would you not do it with more application of spirit? If it is to obtain pardon for your sins, where is that humble and respectful posture, where are those tearful and crushed

---

[51] Such critiques of irreverence in churches are very common in Chrysostom's writings, but I have not found this exact quote.

habits, where are those sobs, those tears, those prayers, with which a criminal is accustomed to appear before his judge? Perhaps you present yourself here with the design of showing some gratitude to Him for so many favors that you have received from Him? Perfidious! Eh! In what manner would you comport yourselves there if you had a design to avenge yourself over an outrage and to insult your Master? My God, how good You are, and how admirable is Your patience!

Saint Justin Martyr says that the pagans of his time kept a stubborn silence—these are his words—in their temples, that they placed a veil over their faces in order to hinder themselves from being distracted by any object of attention which they had brought to their prayers.[52] These infidels will someday put us on trial; they will rise up against us in judgment in order to demand justice for our meager religion. "What, Lord!" they will say, "You damn us for having had the misfortune of not knowing You, and there will be some mercy for these impious ones who have dishonored You after having known You?

---

[52] Unfortunately, I have found no similar passage in St. Justin Martyr, though he mentions that pagans, in their temples, imitated Jewish practices in ceremonial washings and removing shoes (*First Apology*, §62). Tertullian also mentions the importance of silence in regards to mystery religions (*Apology*, §7), though this is regarding the content of the mysteries themselves, not the believers' conduct in the temple.

It is true that they have trampled the idols underfoot, but have they had more respect for You Yourself? If one has deemed it so great a crime for us to have rendered some honors to the false gods, is it a less enormous crime to have despised the true God? We have rendered a cult to creatures which was not due to them, but how many of Your Christians are more culpable for having refused You the respects which were due to You by so many titles? If we have adored naught but the phantoms of divinity, at least we have been true adorers, and one cannot deny that we have treated our profane ceremonies holily; these had holier Mysteries, and they have profaned them. Who merits a more severe judgment, we who has feared powerless gods, or those who have mocked all of Your power? We who have revered the presence of blind masters, or those who have dared to sin in Your eyes; we, finally, who have been religious unto superstition, or those who have been impious unto sacrilege?" And will there be anything juster than these reproaches? What will we have to answer to this comparison? What could Jesus Christ answer? Nothing at all, except that He will satisfy them by punishing you.

Through our immodesties, we give cause for thinking that we do not believe; this is a witness that we render against the truth of our Faith; it does not imply that we do not believe, but rather that all of our belief is only a fable. According to the thought of Saint Cyprian, *Blasphemiam ingerit religioni, quam colit, qui quod profitetur non ante omnes impleverit, ne christianitas videatur fallacia [He casts blasphemy upon the religion he worships, he who does not fulfill what he professes before all, lest Christianity appear a fallacy].*[53]

You go to church, and you believe that this is enough to appear Catholic; the first Christians sometimes entered into the temples of the false Gods in order to mock their impious mysteries, in order to shatter and overturn their statues: has one ever thought to say that they were idolaters because of this? You go to church, it is true, but if you went into the mosques of the Turks and you committed the same irreverences there, you would expose yourselves to being stoned by those infidels. The Huguenots, in the last century, went into Churches, but in order to pillage them, in order to profane them, in order to bar entry to Catholics. This is what immodest Catholics do a little while later; they come there in order to decry the most holy ceremonies, in order to authorize, by their actions, all that Calvin taught his Sectators: in a word, they go there in order to desolate them with as much more malice as one has

---

[53] This is from a treatise, *On the Singleness of Clerics*, falsely attributed to St. Cyprian of Carthage (PL 4:841C–D).

less reason to expect a similar outrage on the part of a Catholic; the sacrileges of the heretics could, at the most, only hinder the exercise of our religion, while the others labor to extinguish it in spirits.

What a misfortune, lovable Jesus! if, when Christians go into Your churches in order to nourish themselves with that flesh which inspires purity and modesty, in order to drink of that wine which engenders virgins, they find objects there which awaken the passions, which rekindle immodest fires in their hearts. Where, then, must Your elect henceforth retire to? What! Will they find what they flee everywhere in this world? Will they be constrained, in order to avoid it, to forbid themselves from our churches, as they have been obliged to renounce the theater and to ban themselves from assemblies? "The churches," says St. John of Damascus, "are like ports which God has established in villages": *Tanquam portus in mari, sic Ecclesias in urbibus fixit Deus.*[54] Today, there is no

---

[54] The quote is actually by St. John Chrysostom; see his *Sermon on the Baptism of Christ*, §1 (PG 49:363): "Do you not know that, like harbors in the sea, God has set up churches in the cities, so that, fleeing there from the surge of life's tumults, we would enjoy the greatest calm?" A variant of this quote, though, is found in an anthology of scriptural and patristic texts whose editing is ascribed to St. John Damascus, the *Sacred Parallels* (§E.6; PG 95:1433D–1436A).

longer surety even in those ports, and it is in vain that one goes there to seek calm after the agitations which the cares and affairs of the world cause. What does it serve that the entrance of our churches be closed to the demon, according to St. Cyprian, if he sends to us there more dangerous tempters than he himself is?[55]

Our immodesties in the churches exposes us to the reproaches that Tertullian gave to the pagans: "You punish us for a crime for which you are culpable; we despise your gods, and do you not despise them yourselves? Do you not do more honor to the statues of the emperors than to those of Jupiter? If your Gods saw the crimes that are committed in your temples, if they saw that trysts are arranged there, that it is there that one makes arrangements to accomplish the adulteries that one has planned, who, do you think, they would have less reason to be offended by: you, or us strangers?"[56]

---

[55] Per Ravier, this is based on an idea in St. Cyprian's *Book on the Habit of Virgins* §XX, where he condemns virgins who, after consecration, betray their virginity: "Thus the enemy fighter slips in, through his arts; thus, through deceitful snares, the devil secretly surprises" (PL 4:459A).

[56] This quotation paraphrases a number of passages in Tertullian; see his *Apology*, §24: "And, on the contrary, the condemnation will fall upon you, who, worshiping a lie, not only neglecting the true religion of the true God, but, furthermore, fighting against it, in truth, you commit the crime of true irreligiosity" (PL 1:416B); §28:

This is why the religionists[57] could reproach us for having done harm in accusing them of irreligion; they could tell you that Christianity is naught but a trick. "Indeed," they say, "you yourselves believe that Jesus Christ is God and Man all together, that He is the King of Glory, that He is your Master and your Judge, and you treat Him so unworthily. If you believed, indeed, that He was in your tabernacles, you who so well understand the rules of civil duty and honesty, you who are so reserved, I do not say in the palace and chamber of great men, but in the very house of your friends, if you believed, I say, what you tell us, would you dare to thus lose respect for your God? We have naught but disdain for your sacraments, and do you yourselves not teach us to despise them? Are you not very unjust to treat us as heretics if we have no faith in the real presence of

---

"This leads, then, to the second accusation, of offending a more august majesty: indeed, you regard Caesar with greater dread and more fervid fear than Olympian Jove himself, and with merit, if you knew it" (PL 1:436A); §15: "If I add the rest—which no less than the consciences of all recognize—adulteries planned in the temples, prostitutions performed among the altars, lechery consummated in the very dwellings of many temple-keepers and priests, under the very priestly headbands and hats and purples, with incense smoking—I do not know but that many of your gods would complain about you rather than the Christians" (PL 1:363A).

[57] That is, the Huguenots, the French Calvinists.

Jesus Christ in the Eucharist, which is nearly the only point that divides us, but are not you truly impious if you persuade us of this, and ought you not to frankly avow that this real presence is a wholly extravagant reverie? And, when you avow this, you would say nothing more than your conduct has already taught us." What would you say, little impious one, you who do glory in all these disorders, if a Huguenot gave you these reproaches and proved to you, by this, that he is more orthodox than you are: what would you say to him?

The heretics are like the Jews who did not want to recognize Jesus Christ; irreligious Christians are like the soldiers who recognized Him in beating Him and spitting in His face. There are those who do not go to church except to be seen: witness their care in dressing themselves, adorning themselves to go to church; it is as if Saint Magdalene had put her jewels back on in order to go assist at the crucifixion, and how dare you appear in your most splendid clothing in our churches, where you received Baptism, where you yourselves were clothed with Jesus Christ, where you made a vow to hold all the vanities of the world in horror, but very far from being ashamed of appearing there in this state, the majority of Christians would be ashamed to appear there in another state; they would not go to our churches if they were not adorned;

they adorn themselves only for this reason, in such a way that they do not wish *to go* there when they have not had the leisure of preparing themselves. *An saltatura ad Ecclesiam pergis? An in Ecclesia lasciviæ oblectamenta quæris? [Do you come to the Church to dance? Do you seek lustful pleasures in Church?]*[58] What are you planning, libertine, with this primping and this nudity? Is it not enough that one suffers these things from you at the ball or at the comedy? What! The altar itself, will it not be an asylum against the murders which you commit through your looks and through your scandalous vanities? What a misfortune, my divine Master! If, after having defended ourselves from the snares of the demon, our brother Christians lay out more dangerous ones for us through their luxury and their little modesty, if we receive poison through their eyes in the same place where we would seek the antidote! Saint Paul, because of this, prohibits women from showing themselves unveiled in the churches, because of the angels, that

---

[58] See St. John Chrysostom, *Homilies on 1 Timothy*, 8.1: "What do you say? Do you approach to beseech God, and are you crowned with gold and braids? Certainly you did not come to dance? Certainly not to partake in weddings? Certainly not to attend a parade? There the gold, there the braids, there the costly garments have their time; but now there is need for none of them" (PG 62:541). The Greek word for "wedding" can also refer to the marital act itself, which is how the translation La Colombière quotes interprets it.

is to say, the chaste and pure souls who pray there with them. *Ideo debet mulier velamen habere supra caput suum, propter Angelos [Therefore, a woman ought to have a veil over her head, because of the Angels]* (1 Cor 11:10), that is to say—St. Ambrose, St. Anselm, St. Thomas say—*propter Episcopos et Sacerdotes [Because of Bishops and Priests]*.[59]

---

[59] See Ambrosiaster (Pseudo-Ambrose), *Commentary on 1 Corinthians*: "The veil signified power, he calls the bishops 'angels,' as is taught in the Apocalypse of John (Rv 2:1ff). . . . In the Church, she ought not to have a free head, but covered by a veil, because of episcopal reverence; let her not have the power of speaking; since the bishop has the persona of Christ" (PL 17:240C–D). For a commentary on 1 Corinthians ascribed to St. Anselm, see *D. Anselmi Archiepiscopi Cantuariensis…Operum Omnium*, Tomus Secundus (Cologne: Petrus Colinus, 1612), 144: "Let her not have a free head in Church, but covered with a veil, and *because of the Angels*, that is, because of the Priests, the announcers of the divine will." See St. Thomas Aquinas, *Commentary on 1 Corinthians* §613: "*A woman ought to have a veil over her head because of the Angels*. Which, indeed, can be understood in two ways. In one way, about the heavenly Angels, who are believed to visit the congregation of the faithful, especially when the sacred mysteries are celebrated. . . . It can be understood in another way, according to which the priests are called 'Angels,' inasmuch as they announce divine things to the people. . . . Therefore, a woman ought to always have a veil in Church because of the Angels, that is, because of the priests." Ravier notes that these three saints are referenced, in this order, in Cornelius a Lapide's *Commentaria in Scripturam sacram*, Tome XVIII (Paris: Louis Vivès, 1880), 355: "Ambrose, Anselm, St. Thomas understand 'priests and Bishops,' whom Rev 2 calls 'angels,' lest unveiled women provoke them to lust by their form."

This is because, he says, their hair forms a part of their glory, since nature has given it to them in order to serve them as a veil (1 Cor 11:15). What abuse is made of it today!

How ought one to judge a person who dares to flirt in the Church? What will she do in secret, and when she has no one to witness her actions except the accomplices of her crimes?

On Ingratitude

It is necessary to apply oneself in order to know the graces God has given us. If one does this as one ought, one would find so much love in the conduct that God has shown with regard to us that it would be impossible for one not to love Him. I am not astonished that one often has more recognition for the superintendent who pays than for the prince who orders, because, without the good will of the superintendent, that of the prince would be useless, and the prince did not give this zeal to his minister. But God is the author of the good will of those who immediately do us good.

God's intention in doing us good is to bring us to love Him through gratitude, which is the greatest of all goods. Recognition of those who have done us good is as natural a movement as vengeance towards those who have done us evil. We do not want to recognize God as the author either of the good or the evil which comes to us; if we did this, we would love none but God, and we would not hate men.

God asks us for: 1. A recognition of feeling. 2. An effective recognition. The effective one consists in giving a part of our goods to the poor. God imitates the steward of the Gospel; He gives good to certain men so that they might assist Him in His necessity (Lk 16:1–8). What ingratitude! You have all from God, and you do not want to show Him the least gratitude! It does not strike you that the prophecy of Jesus Christ would remain without effect with regard to so many holy mendicant religious, to whom He has promised to give a hundredfold (Mt 19:29), and who have followed the counsel of not thinking of their subsistence? You have the courage to see them at your doors, practicing a humility which draws the eyes of God and of the angels, and to receive them with a barbarous hardness, without being touched by so heroic a virtue! Must one be astonished if, after this, God permits trials and bankruptcies, if He takes away the goods for which you've given Him so little thanks? Where are the marks of your recognition, where are the poor you have clothed, where are the altars you have enriched with the goods you have received from God?

There is nothing as just as recognition towards God. Since He has done so much for us, He has obliged us first (1 Jn 4:19) when we were His enemies (Rom

5:10): all the good that men do to us, we ought to be uniquely obliged to Him for it; it is He Who gave them the means, the commandment, the will for it. One is ungrateful for them, one forgets them, one uses them to offend Him.

The prayers of the saints do not give God the will to do us good, but they are only, and in some way, the cause of the execution of that will, or, rather, they are the means He uses to execute it. It is He Who gives them the will to pray, and not they who inspire Him to do us good.

All worship of God consists in this point, that the soul be not ungrateful for His benefits and for His graces. Recognition is the effect of true humility, which consists in recognizing what we do not have, and we cannot have anything by ourselves. We are all charged with a great burden, either that of our sins or, if God has discharged us of this, of the grace which He grants us through this mercy, which is, indeed, a lighter burden, but yet greater than the first, because of the great recognition to which it obliges us; thus, God charges us in discharging us, He discharges us of our sins and charges us with His benefits. God, holding all the good He has done to the ungrateful as lost, is content with having once lost what He gave them, and He does not want, in the future, to expose Himself to losing again what He has given to persons who have no feeling for His gifts.

"Where were you when I laid the foundations of the earth?" (Job 38:4) As if truth spoke openly to the justified sinner: "Do not attribute to yourself the virtues you have received from Me. Do not raise My gifts against Me; remember where I found you, when, through fear of Me, I cast the first foundations of virtues into your soul. Remember the state you were in when I strengthened you through My love. Have continually in your spirit, then, what you were by yourself if you do not want Me to destroy what I have built here."

Who is he whom the truth has not found in crimes and excess? But we can, afterwards, well conserve what we are if we never forget what we have been. When a man has obliged us: first, at that hour, one shows him one's gratitude through words full of friendship. 2. Afterwards, one looks out for occasions to give him the same, and one is disquieted until one has done it. 3. Recognition is not paying a debt: it is necessary to give something of one's own, and to someone to whom one has no obligation except that of gratitude.

On Intemperance

One complains every day that men relate everything to food, that they only labor for this, that they make it their final end. These are people whose bodies are of no use to the spirit, and while reasonable men complain about having a body which causes pain to the spirit, those would like to be destitute of that spiritual soul which troubles, by its lights, the bestial pleasures they seek. Reasonable men eat to fortify the body, for fear that its weakness be communicated even to the spirit; those eat until they choke the spirit and ruin the body. They do not eat except to eat. You would not want to nourish a beast who did nothing else but eat; you nourish a horse in order to ride it, a bird in order to have the pleasure of hearing it sing, and you only nourish your body in order to give it the brutal pleasure of being full of wine and foods? One does not eat to live, since nothing is so contrary to health as those excesses, those ragouts, and that variety of foods; nothing is so proper for prolonging life and rendering it exempt from illnesses as a frugal and regulated table.

There are few people who do not die from eating too much. *Debitores sumus non carni, ut secundum carnem vivamus, si enim secundum carnem vixeritis, moriemini [We are debtors not to the flesh, so that we would live according to the flesh, for, if you live according to the flesh, you will die]* (Rom 8:12–13). Is it that we are slaves of our body, and that all ought to be sacrificed to that insatiable animal: goods, honor, life itself? Who is the man of good sense, or however little reasonable he be, who would not greatly prefer, if it were possible, to take his nourishment without feeling that flattering and importune lust, as we take the air that we breathe? This food of life, which we incessantly receive and send back through the nostrils and through the mouth, has no taste, no scent, and yet we cannot go without it for a single moment, so necessary is it to us; instead, we sometimes abstain from drinking and eating for quite a long time. How much happier would we be if we thus took the earthly foods, which are given us to remedy our hunger and our thirst, without tasting it or feeling that deceitful sweetness, which is so dangerous a temptation for us? As we take only enough air for respiration as is necessary so that we not die, let us also take nourishment which suffices for our nature, and never with excess.

One ought to take foods as one does medicines; necessity ought to regulate our inclination, to deliver us from the inconvenience of hunger, and not concupiscence, which lays ambushes for us in pleasure, which follows, like a servant, its master, that solacing which we seek in drink and food; thus, we do for this pleasure alone what we ought to do for necessity alone, which is that much more dangerous, since pleasure does not have the same limits as necessity, since, ordinarily, where there is enough for necessity, there is little for lust; this is why we seek to deceive ourselves, persuading ourselves that we owe to our health what we give to the passion of lust.

Lust is the object of concupiscence, of nature, and of grace. Concupiscence regards it as its end, nature as its support; grace as its enemy. Cupidity is the deregulation of nature, bringing it to seek pleasure as its end, in which the vice of intemperance consists. Necessity is the rule of nature, since it makes one take from pleasure what one needs for subsistence, and cuts out the superfluous, and in this the virtue of temperance and of sobriety consists. But charity is the perfection of nature, and it brings us to even cut off—as much as possible—the pleasure which necessity renders legitimate, and this is where the labor of mortification tends.

It is strange that man, on this point, is subject to a passion from which beasts are exempt; they are wrathful, lascivious, etc., but they never take excess in drinking or eating.

The simplest foods are the healthiest; nature is not remiss in the culinary arts in regards to things which are necessary for our upkeep. The foods which are born from the countries in which we live are preferred by doctors to foreign foods. Indeed, what possibility *is there* that God, Who has made antidotes to be born alongside the venoms, Who has provided for animals in the place where they are born, has placed here men who have to go seeking, at the end of the world, for what will preserve the life that He has given them!

The excess of the mouth draws impurity, weighs down the spirit, chokes the intelligence; it dissipates the goods of the poor, for it only cares about the superfluous; it injures the families whom it ruins, and the health which it destroys.

Those who eat most deliciously are those who enjoy the least pleasure from taste and those who are the most exposed to the mortification of this same sense, and in contrast to those who are nourished by common foods, since they, being accustomed to what is rarer, cannot be touched by anything and suffer all that is most common when it happens that they are reduced to this, while the others do not suffer those common foods to which they are accustomed, and extremely taste rare *foods*, when they have them.

Hector Boethius, who wrote the history of Scotland,[60] says that plagues and violent fevers were unknown in that kingdom as long as they held to the country's foods and were content with the simplest seasonings, but what extraordinary maladies were introduced by outsiders' ragouts and foods!

---

[60] Hector Boethius, or Hector Boece (1465–1536), wrote a *History of the Scottish People (Historia Gentis Scotorum)*, first published in 1527, as well as a book of *Lives of the Bishops of Murthlack and Aberdeen*, published in 1522. This topic is particularly discussed in the preliminary matter of the book, in the section "On the Scots' Ancient and Recent Institutes and Mores," in *Scotorum Historiæ a prima gentis origine…* (Paris: Josse Badius, 1527), 17v–20v. There, Boece says that interactions with the British led the Scots to abandon their simple, strengthening diet and adopt the British love of culinary novelty, which sickened the people; if they returned to their ancient virtue of culinary simplicity, the Scots would regain the strength they had lost through gluttony.

On Submission to the Will of God

Sanctity consists in conforming our will to that of God. And this is how Plato proves that there could not be many gods, since there would be no sanctity in the world, our will being unable to be conformed to many different wills.[61]

Judge, by this, if there are many saints, nearly all the world being attached to its own will—even the most devoted. Proof of this is that even those who are *performing* exercises of piety, for the most part, are only pleased with this because it is their own will; indeed, they are disquieted when one draws them

---

[61] The issue of the conflicting wills of the gods is one of the key points of discussion in Plato's *Euthyphro*, though the dialogue ends with the matter unresolved. Socrates points out the error in basing the meaning of "holiness" on what all the gods love or on what pleases all of them, since they contradict each other, but he does not make this into an argument for monotheism. The Neo-Platonists, though, who formed their philosophy based on selected ideas from Plato, centered their philosophy around the divine One.

from it. Many do not know what God wants from them, and they want to not know this; they do not consult either God or men in order to learn this. Some know it, and do not want to do it, and imagine they make up for this fault by doing some other good thing, which does not shock their inclination. What is admirable in these persons is that they ask God every day that He would make them know His will, as if they did not know it. What, then, do you think of deceiving God, being unable to deceive yourself? How does it help you to trick Him? You give alms, but you know well that He wants you to quit that game, those companies.

Do you pretend to render yourself independent of the will of God? That is impossible; God Himself cannot free you; it is necessary to be submitted to it; your will is the only thing that can support the yoke, but at that time, heart and spirit are overwhelmed by it, because there is naught but the will that can bear it without pain.

A man who is well submitted to God is like a good instrument in the hands of God. Naught is necessary but this; this would not suffice for any other worker, however excellent he might be. Now, see the esteem, the use, the very honor that an able worker makes of an excellent instrument; he uses it when he has to do some work of consequence, and not only that, but he preserves it dearly, he does not lend it to anyone, he keeps it in precious cases, he embellishes it as much as he can, etc.

Our repugnance does not change God's orders, but *even* if it could do this, one must not hope for this. It is to your advantage that His will be done and not yours. I find my happiness in the execution of the will of God and in the submission of mine. I will never be happy if the will of God is not done; I will be the most miserable of men if mine does not submit to it.

No empire is so just, so necessary, but no empire is so advantageous and so sweet as that of the will of God; it is advantageous for us that it be done; it is sweet to be submitted to it, because the will of God aims only at rendering us eternally happy, because our submission renders us happy here below. Our passions deceive us and strongly persuade us that our advantage is in things which are extremely pernicious to us. And if we were exempt from every passion, our ignorance would render us incapable of governing ourselves. Do you know everything that could result from each thing? Can you foresee the future? The experience of others teaches us, and our own. How many times are we deceived in our hopes and in our fears? The wisest, who recognize the ruses, the artifices of self-love, consult disinterested persons regarding what is good or bad for them; what more prudent guide could you confide in than God? One abandons his blindness to a doctor since that is his profession and since we understand nothing about it, although he is not infallible in his art, and one deliberates about submitting himself to God, Who does all with reason, with love, Who loves us as things which are His, as children whom He has twice birthed, for whom He has made all creatures, Who has formed us in order to render us happy—that is His end; that is why He would lack wisdom if He did or permitted something which could not be related to that end.

This submission to the will of God frees us from every other yoke, for, as God wills all that happens to us, and when we will all that God wills, nothing happens to us except what we will. One could not oblige me to do what I do not want, because I want all that God permits.

It is a sign of an unsupportable pride to persuade oneself that, in one's own conduct, one has no need to take advice from anyone, and that one has enough prudence by oneself to govern oneself and to determine for oneself what is best.[62] It is necessary to be accustomed to this in a good hour, in little things, to make acts of submission every day with regard to all that God can will which is most irritating, most painful to nature. Add to all this that if you do His will, He will do yours.

A virtuous lady, being asked if, in the diverse perils she had encountered while traveling, she had not always hoped that God would guarantee her *safety*, she said no, but that she had hoped that what gave Him most glory would happen to her, and in this dependence on the divine will, her heart was always tranquil and satisfied.[63]

The will of Jesus Christ is more right than ours; it cannot fail nor err, and yet He blindly submits it to that of His Father. *Non mea sed tua fiat voluntas [Not My will, but Yours, be done]* (Lk 22:42).

---

[62] Compare St. Basil the Great, *Commentary on the Prophet Isaiah*, II.88: "It is seen how hubris is the beginning of arrogance. For he who spits upon others and is led by none—rather, thinking of them as poor, as ill-bred, as unlearned—from this hubris, he is led to think himself the only wise, understanding, well-bred, rich, powerful one, taking contempt as the beginning of arrogance" (PG 30:261C).

[63] Ravier thinks this "virtuous lady" might have been Jeanne Pinczon, better known as Madame du Houx (1616–1677); after the death of her husband, she became a secular Visitandine and a well-known holy woman, with frequent interactions with the Jesuits. A 1713 biography of her named her "the Spouse of the Cross."

On Impurity

There are many libertines who try to persuade themselves, and even to persuade others, that it is not a great sin, that of impurity. Why is it, then, that one hides it with such care, that one blushes at it? That all laws condemn it? That one has so much pain from being accused of it, that one scarcely ever says all that must be said about it for the integrity of a confession?[64] Why this remorse of conscience? Why is it that God punished it so severely: the deluge, Sodom, the sons of Judah, David? Why is it that other pains—blindness, hardness of heart, loss of faith, atheism, the removal of all graces—so often follows similar faults?

Pœnitet me fecisse hominem [It pains Me to have made man] (Gn 6:7): He does not say this after the sin of Adam, nor that of Cain.

---

[64] A confession lacks integrity if mortal sins are knowingly left unconfessed.

Abraham did not dare to ask for grace for the Sodomites, although he had a great desire one would pardon them, as it appears in the eighteenth chapter of Genesis, and Moses asked for it, and obtained it, for the idolaters (Ex 32:11–14).

Saint Bonaventure gives five marks to recognize carnal love, and to distinguish it from spiritual: 1. Long conversations, if they are useless; now, rarely, long ones can be useful. 2. Testimonies of that love through looks, gestures, movements, flatteries. 3. Disquiet in absence. 4. Jealousy. 5. Complacency towards vices.[65]

Must one be astonished if one finds little faith among such corruption? I would be astonished at the opposite. God does not pour out His gifts upon

---

[65] St. Bonaventure, in his *On the Advancement of the Religious*, II.27, actually gives seven indications of carnal love: 1) it talks much of useless things and little of spiritual things; 2) "insolence of gestures and mores," which betray love; 3) "disquiet of the heart, when they are absent"; 4) "impatience toward fellow-lovers," that is, jealousy; 5) "wrath and disorder"; 6) "little gifts and sweet letters of amatory conversation, little feasts and morsels snatched from the beloved's mouth, and whatever else the beloved has touched, or whatever he has used, which are venerated almost as relics, and preserved as a memorial, as an incentive to continual love"; 7) "disordered negligence in vices towards each other." See *S. R. E. Cardinalis S. Bonaventuræ . . . Opera Omnia*, ed. A. C. Peltier (Paris: Louis Vivès, 1868), XII:389–390.

filth, *non permanebit spiritus meus [My spirit will not remain]* (Gn 6:3).

Aristotle calls the passion which brings one to impurity a kind of epilepsy. The Fathers call it "sin" by antonomasia.[66] Saint Augustine says that this passion is one of the greatest evils which the disobedience of Adam has brought us.[67]

The passion, among them all, to which we have most inclination, and against which we have need of most succor, is that to which we are borne by a thousand means: all the theaters, all the poems, all the songs, the habits made against this vice are today made to favor it, the ladies in whom God has not inspired much natural modesty, except to defend themselves and to render themselves venerable to men, etc. The song which has been made only for ears refers to this passion. The ancients were chaster in their books, in their verses.

---

[66] A rhetorical device in which an epithet or phrase takes the place of a proper name; the more general "metonymy" would seem more appropriate here, as it simply means referring to a concept or thing with the name of something associated with it. A better example of antonomasia might be how medieval authors called acedia "the noonday demon."

[67] A common theme in Augustine; Ravier points to *City of God*, XIII.13 and XIV.17.

It takes away a man's repose, honor, virtue, and reason. Proof that it takes away reason is that it brings one to excess, to incredible extremes: David, Sampson, Solomon, Henry VIII. One returns to this passion with pain.

To avoid it, it is necessary to avoid conversation with persons of the opposite sex and keep on guard against pretexts. One says that it is spirit, virtue, conversation, etc. But all of that in a man, if you are a man, would not have the same effect.

ON VAINGLORY

Although there is nothing in the world more despicable than vainglory, it is, however, necessary to avow that it is not an enemy to despise. One has said a hundred times that it is a thing much more fragile than glass, but this does not stop the most established virtues shattering against it every day as if against the most redoubtable shoal. It resembles nothing so much as wind, to which it has so often been compared (Eccl 1:14), since, being the slimmest and lightest thing in the world, it does not stop shattering the firmest buildings and uprooting the tallest cedars. One could say that, of all the vices, there is no other which has stopped so many souls on the path to piety, no other which has plunged so many from the highest perfection into tepidity and even into disorder; the other vices combat only one virtue, this one attacks them all, and what is completely particular to it is that, instead of growing weaker in the measure that they become stronger, it fortifies itself with them, in some way, men are never more exposed to vainglory than when they have more true merit.

The necessity of obeying can be sweetened in many ways, be it by the use which he who commands makes of his authority, be it by the advantages that he who obeys finds in obedience. There is little power more absolute than that of a father over his children; yet a father uses his power with so much love that, however little docility and good nature the children have, they scarcely feel the yoke that they bear. This same father exercises a much more rigorous dominion over his domestic servants, and nevertheless, they willingly submit themselves to him in light of their salary, which they have agreed upon, but it is necessary to avow that dependence is something a bit rude when he who can command demands very painful services, and when he who ought to obey can hope for no recompense for his services. This is, Messieurs, the unfortunate condition to which all slaves are reduced, and it is to this that all those who let themselves be overtaken by the desire for vainglory voluntarily reduced themselves.

The world is a band of children who scarcely know how to discern good from evil. It is a confused mass of persons of diverse characters and of diverse tastes, the majority of whom have no knowledge, nor virtue, nor conduct, nor judgment; one is blinded by his pride, the other by his avarice; ambition has reversed this one's spirit, lust has changed that other into a beast; one scarcely finds, in any of them, any shadow of true reason; they are all senseless, they who believe themselves wise, and each of them judges himself capable of governing the others, although they do not know how to govern themselves.

Vainglory is a monster with many heads, each of which has a different figure and its own particular movement, but all of which are bizarre in their figures and all of which are moved by the least wind. It is a tyrant given over to all kinds of vices—impious, wrathful, unjust, envious, pitiless—which loves itself much, and which loves none but itself. What blindness, to hasten to gain the approbations of these children, of these senseless ones! What shame for a Christian to make all his glory consist in receiving the praises of this blind, inconstant, vicious judge, whom Jesus Christ has so solemnly condemned, and who has so unjustly condemned Jesus Christ!

What a project, to acquire glory, to want to content so great a number of persons, among whom you scarcely find two who have the same sentiments, among whom you scarcely find even one who has reasonable sentiments! If you dream of pleasing only a single man, you do not stop me from pitying you greatly, for in the end, this design will expose you to a thousand cares, a thousand fatigues, a thousand pains of body and of spirit. It is necessary to study the sentiments, the inclinations of that man; it is necessary to conform oneself to his humor, to wipe away his sorrows, to support his weaknesses, to hide his rages, to regulate oneself based on his conduct, however unregulated it could be, to sacrifice one's leisure, one's goods, one's liberty, and, sometimes, even one's life.

My God! Is there some man upon earth who could merit this from another man? Is there a single one in it who could pay us for so great a sacrifice? No, Lord, there is naught but You Who are worthy of this, and there is naught but You Who could recompense us worthily for this.

A woman who puts it into her head to be agreeable, does she not spend all her life in a continual constraint? What does she not do, what does she not suffer, in order to preserve I know not what beauty, which she believes necessary for her design? There are precautions to take with regards to this at all times, in all seasons; she takes them, however painful, however sorrowful, however contrary they be to her pleasures and to her other

On Vainglory

inclinations; if she has to get dressed, it is an affair—why do I say, "an affair"? It's four or five hours of torment and of torture, for what torment does she exercise upon that body, upon that head, upon that hair, before all that done to satisfy vanity? She never spends her time more badly than when she is in some company where all the world diverts itself. She dreams of naught but making herself noticed, sometimes through her words, and sometimes through her actions; it is necessary to please both that cheerful person, whom a too greatly serious person might shock, and that severe one who would be scandalized by too much cheer; it is necessary to affect virtue in sentiments, sweetness in bearing, delicacy in spirit, and, above all, much naiveté, and a great separation from all affectation. She is a machine, like her body, all of whose movements must be studied, in order to make her go satisfy all the spectators; there are procedures to follow for her voice, there are some for her mouth, for her eyes, for her arms, for a hundred other little cares that I don't know about, and which I want to be eternally ignorant of; whatever they be, there she is, very much occupied *in them*, and one must not be astonished if so many cares take all liberty and all feeling of pleasure away from her. I want you to see what state her heart is in upon her return from an assembly, for which she prepared herself throughout a whole day, and about which she was filled with the most beautiful hopes in the world; things did not go as one would hope: one did not dance as usual, one did find the humor to speak, one was not lucky in repartees, one was embarrassed during a conversation, one expected to receive more honor, more friendship from some person—another drew all eyes and all indulgences: this is a grief, this is a bitterness that one brings back home, and which the domestic servants ordinarily notice more than they want to. A simple look, a hair from the holy Spouse, that is to say, a good thought, a good desire, suffices to win the heart of God for her, to draw upon her the admiration and the applause of all of paradise. *Vulnerasti cor meum in uno crine colli tui, in uno oculorum tuorum [You have wounded my heart with one hair of your neck, with one of your eyes]* (Sg 4:9). But, in order to make oneself loved or considered by the world, one needs many other cares and other fatigues.

Hypocrites are miserable and, nevertheless, unworthy of all compassion; they are, doubtless, very miserable, since they feel all the thorns of the cross without being able to hope to taste its fruits, since they renounce sanctity after having paid all the costs which turn others away, since they go into hell by the narrow

On Vainglory

way, by the very path of paradise. But, all miserable as they are, they are, however, very unworthy of pity, since, voluntarily embracing all that is most off-putting in virtue, without embracing *virtue* itself, they seem to hate in it only what is most lovable, and to cut off all the pretexts that others can find in the difficulties with which it is surrounded.

One does much more for vainglory than for one's salvation, and I do not know if the majority of those very ones who live Christianly would judge salvation entirely impossible if it required one to subject oneself to all that vanity ordains. I do not speak here of the scribes and of the Pharisees; all the world knows that those false devotees consumed themselves in penances and that they gave the poor the tithe of all their goods.

You pretend that the world admires you, and do you not know that able people admire no one, and that idiots do not even praise things which are truly worthy of admiration, since they are above their stature and since they do not understand them at all? What appears to you more admirable in yourself appears as only very mediocre to all those who know you; there are few people who do not believe that they have as much spirit, as much virtue, as much congeniality as you do, but they deceive themselves; they say, on the contrary, that it is you who flatter yourself (I agree): be that as it may, they are very far from admiring you.

You will tell me, perhaps, that you have a reason for being content with the fruit of your pains, since one praises you indeed, and since one gives you all the marks of an extraordinary esteem, but—my God!—why do you take pleasure in thus seducing yourself? Reflect a little more over what occurs in life, and you will find that those grand marks of esteem, you receive them from very few people; *you will find* that they do not mark as much esteem as you have imagined; you will find that these extraordinary praises are those same ones that one has given a hundred times, that you give them yourself every day to people over whom you make very little fuss. Who does one not praise today, be it in order to draw forth reciprocal praises, be it in order to insinuate oneself into their spirits, since one knows that almost everyone is susceptible to flattery? Have you heard many people praised in their presence about whom one has not said a hundred disadvantageous things when one had the liberty to say what one thought? Am I not the most foolish of all men if I believe myself the only one that one praises in good faith, that one does not blame behind his back, in whose favor one says sincerely what one says to others

On Vainglory 139

only as a mockery or, all the more, in order to acquit oneself of a duty of civility which custom has scarcely rendered necessary?

Do you want to know what you can expect from those whom you try to please? Look a little at what others near you have gained; you are not the only one who hungered for vainglory: nearly all the world runs after the same phantom. Swear to me that if you have not thus far obtained, from those who surround you, as much esteem as you have given them, this was not the punishment for taking all the cares that you took. Now, know, then, that it is, at most, the same thing, that it is much if you are, in the spirit of others, that which they themselves are in your spirit.

We believe we give, in every encounter, proofs of a strongly singular merit, but believe me, we esteem what we do too much; there are a thousand people, very mediocre in all things, who persuade themselves that they do not do nothing, that they have a particular character of excellence, and that there is not even the least movement of their body which does not distinguish them from common men. Furthermore, do you believe that one keeps watch over all you do in order to notice you? Do you not know that each one thinks only of himself and occupies himself only with himself, that such a one—whom you believe a spectator—plays a comedy on his side and believes that you consider him? What cause for laughter do we not give the demon? It very often happens that in a whole assembly, no one keeps watch over what others do, although each one in particular persuades himself that he draws all looks, and although, thinking of this, there is no person who does not try to play his role well, who does not make forced grimaces in order to arrest the eyes of those pretended admirers. So if, in the end, one notices your actions, it is very dangerous if one does not notice, too, the motive that makes you act. It is difficult to hide a great desire for pleasure for a long time; one is not always on his guard; passion has a thousand secret exits through which it reveals itself, despite us, and when we think of it least. Now, you well know the disdain that one has for all those who want to be praised and who have no other aim but that. It is strange, but it is nevertheless true, that in order to not displease the world, it is necessary to hide from it the design one has of pleasing it; it only considers those who do nothing for its consideration; you have labored much for it: if it recognizes that it is for itself that you have labored, it holds itself aloof from all that it could owe you for your services.

Dormierunt somnum suum viri divitiarum, et nihil invenerunt in manibus suis [Men of riches have slept their sleep, and they have found nothing in their hands] (Ps 76:5). This is very sad, that such wise, such regulated, such reserved persons, who have escaped even suspicions, who, to all appearances, ought to have been charged with spiritual riches, *viri divitiarum [men of riches]*, that these persons, I say, are found, at death, with hands empty of good works, not one holy[68] action, not one very straight or very pure intention, the love of glory having taken all away or corrupted all. But what will be their confusion on the day of judgment when God will uncover their shame and their folly before all the earth, when, the true saints taking their place at the right hand of the Savior, this man, who has lived with so great a reputation for justice and for integrity, will be seen among the band of thieves, and that lady, so delicate over everything that regards modesty, will be found mixed up with the prostituted women? What, Lord! You do not call those persons who have lived with so much honor and probity, whose conduct has always been irreproachable, who have never given cause

---

[68] The first edition reads "healthy" (*saine*), but later editions alter this to "holy" (*sainte*). Ravier retains the first edition's reading of "healthy" (372).

for the least conversation, whom one has proposed as the idea of what one calls "honest people" in the world? *Amen dico vobis, receperunt mercedem suam [Amen, I say to you, they have received their reward]* (Mt 6:2), "those people," Jesus Christ will say, "have already received their recompense in another life; they have had nothing in view but honor, but I know not what reputation in which they have made the sovereign good consist; as I have had no part in all their labors, they ought not to expect my kingdom: *receperunt mercedem suam [they have received their reward]*."

The demon tries to corrupt good works, which he could not hinder, through vainglory, as Pharaoh, being unable to render the Jews sterile, made them suffocate their children at their birth, or, at least, at the moment they appeared (Ex 1:16). Evil intention is like those midwives who suffocated the children at the same time that they drew them from their mother's womb, and vainglory is like those guards who drowned those who had escaped the Egyptian midwives once they had discovered them. This is why it is necessary to hide them, like the mother of Moses, *quæ concepit et peperit filium, et, videns eum elegantem, abscondit eum [who conceived and bore a son, and, seeing him elegant, hid him]* (Ex 2:2).

Our victories are with the arms which the demon uses to vanquish us, taking further occasion to inspire us with pride. One labors much, one gains nothing, one loses all, one becomes a slave of the world, a slave labors without relaxation, all the fruit of his pain is his master's, one runs after smoke which one does not grasp, one abandons treasures which one had in one's hands, one hastens to please men and God, one, however, does not please the former and one displeases the latter. One can say that, of all foibles, there is none other which has so hindered men and women from sanctifying themselves; one uselessly loses one's life, for one thinks of naught but pleasing the world, one spends half the day primping and dressing, one does for the world all that the saints did for God, without the sweetnesses they had, and even with great griefs, with great disquiet, the world being composed of many bizarre, opposed, disquieted, ill-fitting, irritating heads.[69] One even makes God serve the world when one publishes His graces, when one uses them to acquire a vain reputation, one glories in doing evil by an action one blushes at after having done it. On

---

[69] Perhaps a reference to one of the many-headed beasts of Revelation, such as the dragon (Rv 12:3), the beast from the sea (Rv 13:1), or the scarlet beast with the woman on its back (Rv 17:3).

the contrary, one blushes for having done good, and one draws vanity from it when one has done it.

It is strange that God so exactly and so liberally pays for all that one does only for Him, and that one takes so little pain to please only Him; the world, on the contrary, does not pay when it notices that one labors for it, and each hastens to satisfy it, and to see it as the judge of all the good that one does. The yoke of the Lord would be unbearable if it demanded all that one does for the world.

One surmounts, one weakens all other enemies through the practice of the virtues, and even through this, vainglory fortifies itself.

Ah, what! It will never be enough for me to have God and all the world as the witness of my actions; I will not be content if, alongside the Most Holy Trinity, besides Jesus Christ and Mary, besides all the angels and all the saints, a heap of miserable blind men and idiots does not also enter into the theater, before whom I wish to act!

"Let all the earth blame me," said an ancient, "provided that Cato praises me; I will take no pains to console myself for the judgment of all the rest of the world, when I have Cato for me."

The world is full of those people; you see what others around you have gained, what you esteem in them; have you only thought of them? Have you reflected on their actions, on their words? All the world is an actor in this comedy, and if someone casts his eyes upon his companion, it is in order to censure him, to envy him, to slander him. This man whose esteem you seek thinks, at the same time, of winning yours; one is blinded to the good, one does not notice it. He imagines that everyone thinks of him, speaks of him, be it good, be it bad, and no one thinks of him. Do you imagine that there are few people who do not esteem themselves at least as much as you esteem yourselves, and that, consequently, they are very far from admiring you?

It is necessary to edify one's neighbor, I agree, but beyond that, it is necessary to do it with a very pure zeal for the glory of God, it is necessary to hide all that one is not obliged to do in His presence and to imitate Jesus Christ, Who detached Himself from the earth in the sight of His disciples but Who was immediately covered with a cloud in order to veil the sight of His triumph from them (Acts 1:9).

On Humility

We submit ourselves to God and to men for love of God, and the reason for this submission is the sincere and true thought one has that one is inferior to others. Knowledge of God, of neighbor, of ourselves, and the comparison that we make between us and others, in things of such different kinds as between their virtues and our vices, support us in humility; these same things inspire it in us if we lack it. Furthermore, it teaches us to despise the things of earth and to love eternal *things*, as a person who aspires for a crown pays no heed to the other honors which are below that one, and he not only despises them but blushes if one offers them to him.

How is it that one could have pride in oneself, that one could prefer oneself to others, or despise someone, not knowing what God's predestination is? How does this thought alone not give us a profound veneration for the least of our brethren? Your sentiments are, perhaps, very opposed to those of God.

The memory of what one has been and of what one could be serves to humble us greatly.

If you esteem yourself for something, you are nothing, you are in illusion, for true sanctity is always accompanied by humility. Saint Peter came to perform a miracle when he said: *Exi a me, quia homo peccator sum [Depart from me, for I am a sinful man]* (Lk 5:8).

Devotion without humility: a worse disposition than vice with regards to grace, since grace easily leads a wicked man to be humble, and the demon easily leads a vain man to be wicked. Witness the Jews and the Gentiles.

Devoted converts ought to be supported in great feelings of humility; otherwise, *they are* very subject to letting themselves be seized by pride. As, when one loses the use of one sense, the others grow stronger, so when one departs from one vice, some other one gains new forces from this; it is in view of this that the devoted Gerson says that he does not want consolation which would steal compunction from him, no ravishment which would ravish humility from him. When one is holy, one is very humble.[70]

---

[70] See Thomas à Kempis, *The Imitation of Christ*, II.X.3, in *De Imitatione Christi: Libri Quatuor* (Turin: Marietti, 1927), 107: "I do not want a consolation which would take compunction from me, nor do I desire a contemplation which would lead to elation."

On Humility

True grace acts like nature: all the parties act equally and in proportion, the one to the other.

Truly good people think little of others, and they only occupy themselves with their own imperfections; others, on the contrary, attach themselves to the practice of virtue, not because it sanctifies them, but because it distinguishes them. It is not that wanting to live according to the maxims of the Gospel, one could be hindered from distinguishing himself, because of the world's corruption, but it is necessary that one not do it for this reason; it is necessary to hope that all the world does its duty, and one mark that is sought in devotion is that one has less care for essential things and that one attaches oneself to the least observances.

Sin gives a great reason for humbling oneself; I have fallen into sin, I have fallen into sin voluntarily, with knowledge, with malice, and I have had very little part in my conversions: it is God Who began, Who awoke me, Who pushed me, Who carried me, Who forced me, in some way; the demon has sinned only once, and he is so horrible that if God permitted us to see him with all his ugliness, we would lose spirit and life at that

---

The Imitation was originally published anonymously; among the writers it was formerly ascribed to was Jean Gerson (1363–1429), a famous French theologian and preacher.

hour. What reproach does he—and all the damned, with the demons—not make to God regarding our life, because we are not damned like them, having, for the most part, merited more or as much as them! A man who was in danger of being hanged, and who did not escape the cord except through the pure mercy of the prince, has great reason for humbling himself.

Adam, having sinned, hides himself and does not dare to show himself; Cain conceals himself from the eyes of his father; his sin humbles him, since, in the first days, one was not yet familiarized with crime. A man who knew that all the world hates him, with justice, would be able to have none but the lowest feelings about himself, and pride in such a man would be folly and not vanity; we are convinced that sin draws the hate of God—which is so just, so luminous, so good—upon us: how much ought this hate to humble a sinner, since, although God has been hated by men, although He has been insulted by them, He can hate nothing but evil. He hates the demons: now, there is nothing—neither in the demons, nor in the damned—so horrible as what is in the soul which is in sin; I am as hateful to God as all the demons, as all the damned, and I cannot humble myself.

If God revealed to you today that you were the greatest saint there is in the world, you ought to be humble, as a peasant woman whom the king had dressed as the queen would not dare to appear. If He revealed to you your perseverance in the good until the last moment of your life, you ought to be even humbler, and confused about having received so many goods without merit, and being unable to recognize them in any way; if, after this, I were proud, I would be lost, for I would have no pity from God.

Vice is, in some way, a disposition towards humility.

Nothing is so opposed to faith as pride; this is why God has said, *Absconditi hæc a sapientibus et precedentibus,*[71] *et revelasti ea parvulis [You have hidden this from the wise and the superior, and You have revealed it to the little ones]* (Mt 11:25). This is why, per the witness of Jesus Christ, the idolaters, the towns of Tyre and Sidon (Lk 10:14), those of Sodom and Gomorrah (Mt 10:15), were more susceptible to the Gospel, because of their pride.

---

[71] The first edition has *precedentibus*, "from the superior," "from the surpassing," or "from those who excel"; later editions correct it to *prudentibus*, "from the prudent," which matches the Vulgate. I think La Colombière's erroneous quotation, though, fits his meaning well, as the "superior" are wont to be even more proud than the "prudent."

ON ADVERSITIES

Scripture says that the three children were not injured nor afflicted in any way by the fire: *Et non tetigit eos omnino ignis, nec constristavit eos [And the fire did not touch them at all, nor afflict them]* (Dn 3:50).[72] This is a great miracle; but just men in adversity make us see a greater one: *Teitgit eos ignis nec constristavit eos [The fire touched them but did not afflict them].*

There is as much difference between a man who acts for God and another who suffers, and the glory which they render to God is as different, as *the glory* which He receives from the sun, when it goes from setting to rising, is different from that which He receives from the same star when it stops in the midst of its course (Jo 10:12–13).

---

[72] In many modern translations, such as the RSV-CE, a large portion of Daniel 3—found in the Greek (Septuagint) version, but not the Hebrew—is separated out from the rest of the chapter, with its own verse numbers; in such numbering, this verse is v. 27 of that separate section.

There is no other way either to save the sinner nor to sanctify the just; it is necessary to cure that wicked Christian of the love of the world, it is necessary to cure the lax and imperfect Christians of the love of himself, in order to put the first on the way to salvation and the latter on the road of perfection: adversity alone can perform both these marvels. You render all other ways useless, either through continual attachment to pleasure or through focus on affairs; God does not speak in *social* circles, and one does not hear Him there. Affairs give no leisure for reflecting on salvation; one is drunk with vanity and happy successes; that woman's beauty has gone to her head: speak to her of anything else, you won't be heard. To save her, she must be disfigured.

Furthermore, it is certain that we all have a foible which hinders us from going to God for good, something which we hold back from sacrifice; "it is nothing," says Saint Teresa, "but this nothing is an obstacle to great things";[73] you could well cure yourself, but

---

[73] This is a common theme in St. Teresa, though not in these exact words. See, for instance, St. Teresa de Ávila, *Way of Perfection*, 19.3, "And I say again that these things should not appear little to you; that if you do not cut them out with diligence, what was nothing today will tomorrow, perhaps, be a venial sin; and it is so hard to stop that if you leave it, it will not stay alone, and *it will become* a very evil thing for the congregation"; see also *Foundations*,

you do not have the courage, or you don't even know where the ill is. It is necessary that the surgeon, when you think of him least, stab his lancet very far into living flesh and pierce the ulcer hidden at the base of the entrails, without which, you would live in languor.

Is it not true that, from the time you were God's, you had not a little resolved yourself to quit that game, that friendship which is not criminal, but which shares your heart, that love for vainglory and for praise? You well feel a part of the evil that it does to you, but the sole thought of healing frightens you, since it is so near your heart that one cannot bring it the necessary remedy without a violent and painful operation. Your confessor sees the evil well, but he flatters you, since he sees well that he would afflict you in making you recognize it, and that he would not be able to make you accept his advice afterwards; it is necessary, then, that God permit a malady, a confusion, a death. While that child lived, he occupied a part of your thoughts and your affection; God wants to have it completely whole: it is necessary that he die.

27.11, "See how very small things open the door for very great ones." See Santa Teresa de Jésus, *Obras Completas*, ed. Efren de la Madre de Dios and Otger Steggink, 8th ed. (Madrid: Biblioteca de Autores Cristianos, 1986), 288–289, 773.

That rich man is surrounded by temptations, by flattery, by honor, by charges, by pleasures; there is naught but adversity which could awaken him. God could well open for us a new path to paradise. It is true, but if He has not done so, do you believe that this was without reason, or that He had no other *reason* than the pleasure of seeing you miserable and suffering? He has judged that it was to your advantage; He has foreseen that you will eternally thank Him for having followed this conduct with regards to you, that you will love Him more for it; if this is so, why is it that a thing for which you will bless Him, for which you will eternally rejoice, casts you into sadness and brings you to murmur against His divine providence?

It is a great mercy of God when, instead of punishing the soul that has sinned, He strikes the body, whose wounds could be useful; this is like when one, in human justice, reduces corporal punishment to a fine.

The malady humbles, makes one feel human infirmity and the grandeur of God, Who is outside the touch of all evils, Who is eternal; it makes one know what one is in oneself; through the need one has of very inferior persons, it places us, in some way, below all those who have more health than us, wherefore, in this state, one often envies the fortune of a poor peasant who enjoys perfect health in the midst of the travails to which his condition and his poverty engage him. One is no longer so fierce, nor so insolent; one learns compassion, recognition, etc. The malady recalls the memory of sins, and it makes one comprehend their malice through the severity of the punishment.

I am astonished that it takes so much pain to be persuaded that one can be happy in adversity, seeing how one has seen so many miserable persons in the greatest prosperity. If there are invisible evils, is it impossible that there are secret sweetnesses?

When God sends us crosses, He does it through the same principle of charity through which He willed that His only-begotten Son be crucified for us. "We are members of Jesus Christ, from which it follows," says Saint Augustine, "that, as all that He endured on the day of His passion and His death, we have endured in His Person, so, now, all that we suffer, He Himself suffers in our persons."[74]

---

[74] See St. Augustine, *Explanation of the Psalms*, On Psalm 62 [63] §2: "Since, therefore, we now know the head and the body: He is the head, we the body. When we hear His voice, we ought to listen with both head and body; since, whatever He suffered, we also suffered in Him; since, too, what we suffer, He also suffers in us" (PL 36:749).

Jesus Christ is the witness, the companion, and the author of our sufferings. He sees the evil that you suffer, He suffers the evil that you suffer, He makes the evil that you suffer. If we were enlightened enough to see our true advantages, we would ask for adversity. He even makes the evil which the damned suffer, but He does not suffer it with them.

It is not one of your friends who makes you suffer, no, but it is in the sight of your father, who would not suffer it if it were not useful to you; if it were not advantageous for you to suffer, God, in preventing it, would render Himself useful to you and to your enemy, while, in permitting it, He would not have an end worthy of Himself, this being disadvantageous to both of you. That father who sees his son's skull open suffers more than him, and thus, one must not believe that if it were not really useful to him, he would permit it.

The prosperity of Solomon, although it came from God, had more force to pervert him than his wisdom had to retain him in his duty. Tobias, having lost his eyes by an accident, as all the world knows, his relatives and his allies mocked him, like a man who had lost his alms and his other good works, but he responded to them, *Nolite ita loqui, quoniam filii sanctorum sumus, et vitam illam expectamus, quam Deus daturus est his, qui fidem suam nunquam mutant ab eo* [*Do not speak thus, for we are sons of the saints, and we expect that life that God is to give to those who never change their faith away from Him*] (Tob 2:17–18).[75]

The author of the testament of the patriarchs says of Joseph that he praised God in the place of shadows, that is to say, in prison.[76] Joseph never believed himself more miserable than when he saw himself sold. What prayers did he not make to bend his brothers; what vows did he not offer God to make Him change their hearts! I do not doubt that he asked this with every kind of submission, but if he had obtained it, this would have been a very great misfortune for him. Likewise, when he was put in prison. My God, will we never learn to submit ourselves? *Non ne Deo subjecta erit anima mea? Ab ipso enim salutare meum* [*Shall not*

---

[75] These verses are only found in the Vulgate version of Tobit, not the Greek (Septuagint) version, which most modern translations follow.

[76] The *Testaments of the Twelve Patriarchs* is an apocryphal Jewish or Christian text thought to have been written or finalized in the second century AD; the reference seems to be to *Testaments* XI.1–2, where Joseph recounts his sufferings and how he kept faith in God despite them, and how God saved him. The closest line to what La Colombière is referencing seems to be in XI.2: "For God does not abandon those fearing Him, not in darkness, nor chains, nor afflictions, nor necessities" (PG 2:1125C–1128A).

my soul be subject to God? For from Him is my salvation] (Ps 62:1). Will we never be entirely Yours?

"But I do not become better through this"; if this is so, I pity you, I do not believe that there is a greater mark of reprobation; you are despairing: if this is so, there are few like you. God, Who has permitted this misfortune, could have prevented it, and if it was not useful to you, you should think that He would not have done it, this being easy for Him, He Who, in order to prevent you from being unhappy in the other life, surmounted so many obstacles, suffered so much Himself.

The word of God saves us, but it little serves a man who is in great prosperity; he does not hear it, but once he is in adversity, everything profits *him*, he seeks to be consoled, and there is nothing but God, etc. It distances flatterers, libertines, it draws near, it opens the door to good people, etc.

Adversity is even necessary for the good in order to preserve them from corruption, like salt which consumes and preserves. This is a sign that God loves you and that He wants to be loved by you; He is jealous. He sees that that child has your heart, He wants to take that child away from you; nothing distinguishes love so much as jealousy.

On the Mercy of God Towards Sinners

It is strange that men and Christians have so ill-bent a spirit that the knowledge of the mercy of God leads them to offend Him, even to the point that some deem this a reason why one ought not to write or speak *of God's mercy*, for fear of drawing sinners into impenitence. However, it is the most glorious of His attributes. *Miserationes ejus super omnia opera ejus [His mercies are above all His works]* (Ps 145:9).

The mercy and the sweetness of God's conduct marvelously appear in the manner in which He sweetens the older brother of the prodigal child: He quits the company, He leaves the room, He hears his reproaches, and instead of treating him with haughtiness, He rather wants to give him a reason for His conduct; He flatters him: *Tu semper mecum es, et omnia mea tua sunt [You are always with me, and all of mine are yours]* (Lk

15:31). This is how He acted towards Jonah, who complained about God's pardoning Nineveh; He conquered him through his own sentiments, but lest sinners take a false confidence from this in order to persevere in their crimes—for, from that moment on, they would abuse His mercy, they would offend it, they would even irritate it against them: from that moment, it would become their adversary;[77] mercy does not save those for whom it is a cause of their being damned. Why is it that the mercy of God appears? To inspire in the sinner the desire to return. For that is an effect of the mercy of God, but it is a great mark that there is no longer mercy for a man when he uses it as a reason to not convert.

Spes non confundit [Hope does not confound] (Rom 5:5), but what is hope in a sinner? It is the confidence of a man who repents and who hopes that God will have regard for his repenting. The confidence of a man who does penance because he hopes, but the hope of a man who sins because he hopes is worth no more than despair; it is a false hope, it is a hope which confounds. I hope because God has promised me, and you ought to despair for the same reason, because He has assured you that He will respond, *Nescio vos [I do not know you]* (Lk 13:27).

---

[77] "Adversary," in this case, is used in a specifically legal or juridical sense, meaning the opposed party in a trial.

"*Existimasti iniqui quod ero tui similis, arguam te [You deemed, iniquitous ones, that I would be like you; I rebuke you]* (Ps 50:21). Why do you take the liberty of speaking of My commandments and the promises that I made only to My servants? You praise My mercy, and you base yourselves on the covenant I made with men in making Myself man like them; you hope in the blood by which this covenant was confirmed, and in the promise that I gave to receive, in grace, all those who would have recourse to My clemency, and yet you persevere in your crimes . . . *Existimasti quod ero tui similis [You deemed that I would be like you]*. You believe, then, that I am like you, and that I authorize crime through the impunity that I promise to it? Would this not be to invite men to sin and to draw them into disorder? What wisdom would be that for God, if, while He threatens those who offend Him with an eternity of punishment, He promised them, elsewhere, impunity and the forgetting of all the crimes they could commit?"

The mercy of God ought to hinder you from falling into despair, but I hold you as hopeless if it is an occasion for you to fall into impenitence. If you do not deceive yourself, God would have regulated things very badly, and He would have given a reason for the men who suffer from your unruliness to blaspheme His Holy Name and to condemn His providence. I do not see more despairing people than those who hope in this way. "The mercy of God will save us": how? "In bringing us to love God and in asking pardon from Him": but it is completely certain that it would damn you if it brought you to offend Him. This is why the Incarnation, which is the chief work of mercy, the excess—if one must speak so—of clemency, has lost many who have badly understood the grace which God has granted to men in dying for them; they have believed that they could sin without punishment, and yet God is dead in order to hinder us from falling and, after having fallen, to hinder us from falling into a greater sin by despairing of His goodness, but He is not dead in order to buy the sinner's liberty. He is dead for the salvation of many whom mercy invites to repentance, but He is dead for the loss of many, and it is they who take the liberty of doing everything in view of His merits.

The clemency which Augustus showed towards Cinna snuffed out, in the hearts of all the Romans, the rest of the hate which the love of liberty had brought against that prince who had subjected them.[78] They no longer

---

[78] Cinna (Gnaeus Cornelius Cinna Magnus) was a Roman politician who had been a supporter of Mark Antony in his war with Caesar Augustus; some years after Antony's death, Cinna became part of a conspiracy to assassinate Emperor Augustus.

plotted against his life, and this ease in forgetting injuries of such importance, very far from rendering those who had formed designs upon his person more hardy, made the arms fall from their hands and changed all the aversion that they had conceived against him into love. *Misericordia ejus super omnia opera ejus [His mercy is above all His works]* (Ps 145:9). This is what is greater, more capable of touching us, of bringing us to repentance, so that if this does nothing, you are hopeless.

What mercy! I offend it, and without any other reparation than the sorrow of having done it, He pardons me; I fall again, and He pardons me still; I offend Him every day, and He does not rebuke, His patience is not exhausted by such frequent repeated falls. If I wander away every day, and if I return every day in good faith, He receives me with joy, He pardons me with pleasure, He forgets my perfidy, He gives me all my spiritual goods, with an overflow of graces and merits; there is no less haste to reestablish myself in the first state, after a hundred infidelities, than there was after the first

---

The conspiracy was discovered, but instead of punishing them, Augustus pardoned Cinna and his coconspirators. Cinna then became a close friend and adviser of Augustus. The story became well-known in France through Pierre Corneille's tragedy *Cinna, or, the Clemency of Augustus*, published in 1643, when La Colombière was two years old.

wandering; so many proofs of my looseness do not hinder Him from pardoning me on my word, although I have betrayed Him a thousand times through my inconstancy, although He foresees that, tomorrow, perhaps even today, I will forget His bounties and my resolutions. O truly infinite mercy! O goodness worthy of a God! Woe to those who defied You in whatever state they are themselves reduced to through their malice! Woe to those who, knowing how excessive You are, do not immediately have recourse to You, defer their tossing themselves into Your arms, and prefer to be the objects of divine vengeance and wrath rather than to receive pardon for their offenses! But woe, double woe, and all kinds of woe, to those whom knowledge of Your mercy brings to offend You—my God!—and who are determined to displease You, because You are good!

Saint Theresa had no other subject for meditation in all her life than the mercies of God. This is why one finds many images of her with this phrase: *Misericordias Domini in* æternum *cantabo [I will sing the mercies of the Lord unto eternity]* (Ps 89:1).

What goodness! Jesus Christ is not content with giving men the power to judge and absolve men, but He permits Peter to renounce Him so that He could be still more indulgent; God is touched by our disorders instead of being irritated by them, He runs after the sinner instead of fleeing him, He goes easy on him for fear of giving him confusion; when He draws him back, He makes his sin become useful for him, instead of punishing him for it. One would say that He loses in our wandering away, and that He gains upon our return. He does them more good than before, which is why, according to the remark of Saint Gregory, penitents are ordinarily better servants than those who have not sinned.[79]

---

[79] See St. Gregory the Great, *Book of Pastoral Rule*, III.28: "For often some, returning to the Lord after sins of the flesh, show themselves so much more ardent in good works as they see themselves more damnable by their evil *works*. And often those remaining in integrity of the flesh, when they see that they have less to weep for, consider the innocence of their life to fully suffice for them, and they use no ardent goads to inflame themselves to fervor of spirit. And a life after sin is usually burning with a love more pleasing to God than an innocence numbed by security" (PL 77:106D–107A). In some editions, this chapter is labeled 52 instead of 28.

ON DEATH

One deceives oneself when one says that death is always similar to life; it is, on the contrary, always different from life: it is cruel when it follows a delightful life, it is sweet when it follows a bitter life and one far from the sweetnesses that one can taste upon earth, since it cannot accord with our pleasures, since it troubles and renders them very imperfect.

The thought of death changes the fortune of the man whom it despoils through the disdain for riches to which it brings him; it changes the person of the man whom it disfigures, so to say, through the love of penitence which it inspires in him; it changes him in his sentiments, which it corrects through the true knowledge which it gives him of all things. Death changes all things, and nothing changes after death. The things that appear most immutable—the most established fortune, the healthiest body, and the youngest beauty, the spirits most obstinate in their sentiments: all this changes at death. The most changeable things, like our will, which fears, at each moment, taking on new resolutions, and passing from sin to death, that of God, which lets itself be bent by a sigh or by a tear, the goods and the evils which are naturally changeable and which follow one after the other: all this no longer changes after death.

The thought of death is very necessary, since it leads one to do what one would want to have infallibly done at death, what he will necessarily have to do at death, what one could not, perhaps, do at death, or at the least, what one could not do well then, what one does not do at death except with pain, what one does not do then except by force.

Nothing causes so much pain at death as the poor use of life; this is why one sees so many persons hoping, at death, to have been poor, to have been religious; it is that they believe that, in this state, they would have labored for heaven; they blame on their state what they ought to impute only to their negligence. It is, indeed, an unsupportable pain to see that one has lost a time which will no more return; to go beyond this pain, think often of death, spend each day as you will want to have spent it at death. A pleasant excuse for those who do not want to think of death, because this thought is too sad; it is just as if one did not want to think of defending oneself from poverty, from sickness, from the confusions which threaten us, because these evils are the greatest evils of life.

On Death

All men are so persuaded of the uncertainty of death that they do not want to hazard a part of their goods on the hope of a long life, so ill-founded do they believe this hope; a person to whom one offers an important charge, which he could not pass on to his children, however young he may be, he cares little for it: why? Because, he says, he could die tomorrow, and his silver would be lost. If one sees death come in a year, without having given a certain sum to the prince, one will lose a charge; from the beginning of the year, one bears his tax.[80] But why every year? "Because I could die each year." But why from the beginning, not in three months? "Because I am not assured of living so long a time as that." "But you bear yourself well." It is true, but how many unforeseen accidents happen every day! If the king lifts the Paulette for three months, all the officers are in perpetual fear. These are the sentiments which condemn you, sinner, and regarding which your trial will be held. What do you have to reply? At the

---

[80] This entire discussion relates to the Paulette, a tax first imposed under King Henri IV on December 12, 1604. The tax applied to many government and judicial officers; if they paid the tax, they could transfer their office at will. Thus, by paying the tax, an officer could transfer his office to his son upon death. If the officer failed to pay the tax, or if the king lifted the tax, the officer would lose this right of transfer and, upon the officer's death, the king would have the right to bestow the office on whomever he chose.

same time that the thought of death hinders you from risking a part of your goods, it cannot hinder you from hazarding your eternal salvation: "if I do not pay today, and if I happen to die, my office is lost," and if you do not confess today, and if you happen to die, what will become of your soul and your eternal salvation?

It is important to die well, because it deals with everything and forever, it deals with all your past merits, it deals with your soul and your body, for your death will be the rule of your particular and universal judgment, it deals with procuring all kinds of goods for your soul and for your body and with sparing them hell; if you die badly, even after you have lived very well, all is lost, and this forever.

It is difficult to die well, because it deals not with dying on one's bed, with full knowledge, after having confessed, communed, and received Extreme Unction, all of which can be done in an hour of time—yet it can happen that one dies badly with all of this—it deals with dying in the grace of God, with dying a friend of God; now, it is not as easy to recover grace at death as one thinks, and when one has recovered it, it is easy to lose it, even when one survives only a moment, all the more since, at that time, the demons make all their efforts; when one has to fight an enemy so strong, experienced, and accustomed to conquering, one is challenged by all his forces, one fears. If it was so easy to die well, all the saints would be deceived, since they, so to say, martyred themselves all their lives in order to prepare themselves for a good death.

It is impossible to correct a bad death when this misfortune has occurred, because one does not die twice. Thus Pharaoh, when he pursued the Israelites, entered, without any obstacle, into the sea, through which the people of God had been shielded from his fury. He had advanced on this path, when the cloud, which covered Israel, opens up all at once and with a frightening roar, shoots a thousand lightning bolts, a thousand darts, at that impious king, who recognized too late that he had fallen into the hands of God; he wants to turn his face and turn back on his steps, but the sea has closed off his passage, and he no longer has a way to correct his misstep: he perishes there.[81]

---

[81] It is unclear in Exodus if Pharaoh himself was drowned in the Red Sea; Scripture states that "the chariots and horsemen and all the host of Pharaoh" was drowned (Ex 14:28), and the Lord declared that He would gain glory over Pharaoh and his host (Ex 14:17–18), but in the triumphal song afterwards, Moses only says that "the chariots of Pharaoh and his host" were drowned, not Pharaoh himself (Ex 15:4).

It is strange that Christians are not struck by the discourses one so often gives them about death; it is even more surprising that they are not touched by the sight of death itself; every day they see an image of what they will be in a few days upon the face of their agonizing brothers, they lie down on the sheet in which they will be buried, they sleep in the bed where they are to expire, every day they go to the church where one will carry them some day, they walk upon the ground in which they will rot and be reduced to dust, they hear the same bell sound which will announce their death, and yet—O hardness! O insensibility of men!—they do not stop themselves from laughing, from enjoying themselves; it is a little thing to sin, to offend that same God Who holds their life in His hands. My God! How wise are You to have submitted man to this hard and inviolable law, to have condemned Him to death and to all the circumstances which accompany that frightful separation! What wouldn't we do if we weren't held back by that impenetrable dike, against which all our designs will be broken?

When one gives himself to God, the sight of fifty or sixty years of mortification frightens, but at death, this same sight fills with joy; on the contrary, what joy when one enters into the world, taking possession of a great charge through an advantageous marriage; one sees that all one's life will be spent in honor and in pleasures, but at the hour of death, what reason to hope for paradise, which is promised only to the poor in spirit, and to those who have lived in disdain and in sufferings!

Why is it that having death ceaselessly before our eyes, we think so little of it? It is because we distance this thought from ourselves as much as possible; yet we go towards it, each step draws us to it; when you go to the ball, that many steps bring you closer to death; you can enjoy, dance, run, you go all the same towards death; has one ever seen people on a road who do not think of where they are going?

Sin has introduced death, that is to say, it is a penalty for it, and as one is not contented, in crimes of lèse-Majesté, in confiscating goods, in degrading persons, but one even razes houses, in the same way, the body, which is our house on earth, will be destroyed. Moses was not content with melting down the golden calf and with removing the figure under which it had been adored; he reduces it to powder, and he does not believe the crime of his people has been expiated enough until he had resolved this idol into its first principles (Ex 32:20). This is the punishment which God has established for sin. It is not enough that your body be deprived of that beauty whose idolater you were, that age despoils you of those fragile charms which drew so many adorers, that old age consumes that health which you had abused; it is necessary that death reduce this body to the first elements from which it was composed: mud and dust.

One would blame a man who, seeing his friend at his end,[82] would want to speak to him of an affair of consequence; "Ah, Monsieur!" his assistants would tell him, "he is not in a state to hear you talk of this," and if you insist, you would pass for an indifferent man. To that time, however, one puts off the most important of all affairs, one waits for the last moment to hear a confessor speak to us of salvation.

At death, the impious hopes for all that is absolutely impossible for him, like having lived differently than he had, pushing back the time of his death; he desires to die in order to be delivered from the sorrows he suffers, he would like to not die in order to avoid those which await him; picture to yourself a man whose house is burning, and who is afflicted, from the outside, by his enemies.

In that extremity, the impious loves all that he has hated, he hates all that he has loved, but above all, he hates

---

[82] À l'extrémité can mean "at the end of one's life" or "in dire straits"; consider the phrase "at the end of one's wits." Based on the context of this chapter, here it most likely means the end of life.

both his loves and his hates; he has so much more regret as he finds all that he has hated lovable, all that seemed impossible to him, easy, and he cannot conceive of what little obstacles had stopped him: a ribbon, I know not what, a vile creature whom he preferred to the Creator. His impurities cover him with confusion when he thinks that it is necessary to go spread out all his shame before God, his violences and his cruelties tear him apart, his vengeances fill him with bitterness, his injustices condemn him, his impieties, his blasphemies, the disdain he holds towards God, overwhelm him, destroy him, throw him into a horrible consternation.

The death of the impious is terrible because of the sight of past pleasures and future torments; he is tormented by all that he has tasted of pleasures, he sees that his paradise is past, he is in despair because it was so short, because it was so little sensible. He is overwhelmed by all that he sees of the torments *he is* to suffer, it vexes him to die because his soul, attached to riches and to earth, is like an old tree which holds on with a thousand roots, which it is necessary to cut; these bonds cannot follow it; it is necessary for one to separate them and for them to remain in the earth; he is like Abraham's lamb, caught in the thorns, which stop it, which prick it, which bloody it, which tear it apart, when he goes to draw it out to sacrifice it and, afterwards, burn it (Gn 22:13).

Everything most terrible that an impious man has ever heard said about the judgment, about the wrath of God, about hell, about eternity, all this returns to his spirit at the hour of death and strikes him in a terrible way, although he first mocked it; it is a marvel how much this man, who doubted, who wavered, is persuaded by truths which he had never wanted to believe. Indeed, if there is a state as terrible as that of a man who sees that, in a moment of time, he will be damned or saved, without certainly knowing what will happen, what ought one to think of a man who is assured of his eternal misfortune? No better remedy against the bitterness of death than meditation on this same bitterness; one does not willingly attach himself *to earthly things* when one reflects on the pain that one feels at death from leaving the things to which one was attached.

The death of the just is agreeable through the sight of past evils and of future goods; it is necessary to buy this death at whatever price it be; it is necessary to give all to obtain this precious death; all scruples, all fears are changed, in that moment, into sweetness, into peace, into a certain assurance which God performs.

On Death

Although death is the penalty of sin, it does not stop enveloping the good, but it is not a pain to them, or at the least, it is so sweetened that they desire it, that they taste a great joy in it. Jesus Christ, through the redemption, has taken death away from the soul, and as for the death of the body, which was the second penalty of sin, He took away what was painful in it.

Our body, from the time sin dwelt there, ought to be for us like a poorly-built house, and one whose foundations are ruined; one does not deign to make the least repair to it, one lets it fall apart, bit by bit, until, it being entirely destroyed, one rebuilds it from the foundations, and one corrects all its defects.

The good man, according to Saint John Climacus, is he who does not fear death, and the saint is he who desires it;[83] a person of great sanctity said, at the end of her life, that nothing was capable of contenting her except that single word, *death*; "however, I am," she said, "ready to live as long as God wills, for, there no longer being persecutions of the Church, it is now necessary to sacrifice oneself in life, as the martyrs sacrificed themselves in death."

---

[83] See St. John Climacus, *The Ladder*, VI: "Esteemed is he who, in every way, awaits *death* every day; but holy is he who longs for it at every hour" (PG 88:793D).

ON HELL

Eternity is like a globe which, being applied to the stomach of a miserable person, makes him feel all its weight, although he only touches it at one point; he is overwhelmed by the point of eternity, he suffers all of eternity. Blessed eternity *est interminabilis vitæ tota et perfecta possessio [is the interminable, full, and perfect possession of life]*.[84] Miserable eternity is, consequently, a state where all the differences of time concur and reunite, as if in a point, in order to render a spirit miserable.

What suffering for a damned soul when, from this abyss of eternity, after having burned for a hundred thousand and millions of years, it casts its eyes upon that little portion of time that it will scarcely find at the end of that infinite number of centuries which will have passed since its death! Life appears as naught but a moment, although, looked at very closely, it seems to us, to us who still enjoy it, that all which is in the past

---

[84] See Boethius, *Consolation of Philosophy*, Book V, Prose 6.

is naught but a moment; when one is at the hour of death, however long it will have been, one can scarcely persuade himself that there has been any interval between the day of our birth and that at which we have finally arrived: we seek that life which has passed like a dream, and of which there remain scarcely any traces in our memory; what will it be like when thousands of years have passed since our death, since our children and our children's children were already buried, since our race was lost, since time had ruined the houses that you had raised, destroyed the villages that you have given birth to, overthrown the states in which you lived, since the end of the ages had buried all the universe in its own ashes, since the gates of heaven, as well as those of hell, had been closed in order to never be reopened, and, since that time, a hundred thousand years, a hundred thousand million years will have passed, what will you think? How will that life appear to you? Will you judge, then, that it well merits one to lose eternity in order to enjoy *that life* with the pleasures and honors which accompany it?

What! In order to enjoy some frail pleasures during that moment of life? What! In order to spend in I do not know what honor that atom of time, the idea of which scarcely remains for me, which I almost uselessly seek in the midst of that frightening duration which has either preceded or followed, I am plunged into that darkness, into those eternal flames? What, then, became of those phantoms of glory, of grandeur, of reputation, of immortality, which, at that time, gave me such great cares, which occupied me, which made me forget eternity? What became of those persons whom I loved, those others whose vain judgments, discourses, and power I feared? O God, what blindness, what folly! O God, if I had well wanted to profit from that moment, if I had done what I could do, and what is presently impossible for me, and what will eternally be impossible for me! In that moment, which is the only one I can dispose of, and which will never return; in that moment, which I spent enjoying myself, dancing, laughing, sleeping, doing nothing; in that moment, I had all of my fortune in my hands, I was the master, the arbiter of my good fortune, I had the key of paradise in my power, I had, for thirty or forty years, the liberty of choosing in paradise, in blessed eternity, the richest, the most elevated place; I was offered *the chance* to place myself either among the apostles, or among the virgins, and I refused to do it, and I did not even deign to think of the offers given to me. My God, was I a Christian, was I reasonable, was I a man? Who had blinded me, who had reversed my spirit, who had enchanted me, in a way? Ah, moment, precious moment, short moment, will you, then, return no more, and must you be eternally lost for me? It is already lost for many millions of Christians—alas! even a part of it is lost for you: take guard, lest you lose the rest. If you do not think soon, and as is needed, you will lose it all entirely.

One speaks to us of the fires and flames of hell: they are horrible, they are frightening, but to my sense, it is a little thing in comparison with that regret, with that view of time past, and of the bad use that was made of it. Our spirit will spend all of eternity vividly showing us the vanity of the objects which have turned us away from God, the ease there was for saving oneself. It was so easy to confess that sin; I had so many years of health before my fall, and why did I wait until the hour of death, and why until the day after; where was my spirit, I, who did important things, and who passed for so judicious a man, and one with such good counsel for others? It had only to do what such and such a one had done well. This seems to me something so horrible that if all the other tortures of hell could be separated from it, and if God left it to my choice to either be plunged into that frightful abyss of evils or to be only afflicted with this regret, I would spend a single moment weighing it before choosing the assemblage of all those torments in order to deliver myself from this one, but never will the one be separated from the other: eternally will you suffer, and you will regret the time, the easy means, which you had—which you despised—for saving yourself.

Ah, my God, my good Master, my all-lovable Redeemer, do not damn me, I pray You, through Your precious Blood, through that so tender and so ardent love which You have always showed me. What fruit will You draw, my God, from the loss of that meager creature whom You have formed from mud, and who will soon be reduced to dust? What great glory will return to You, my Lord, when You will have enclosed me, for eternity, in those chasms of fires and flames? Am I a worthy object of so inflamed a wrath, of so long and so cruel a vengeance? But let us ourselves do what is necessary to save us; let us save ourselves, though all the rest will perish.

One would be a fool if one thought of this; one would be a fool by that folly which is only *folly* in the eyes of the senseless world, and which, before God, is high and sovereign wisdom; do you know what would make me a fool if I attached myself to wanting to understand it? It is to accord the life of a sinner and belief in hell; this is why it can happen that you believe there is a hell, an eternity of pains, and that you live in continual peril of falling into it; it is that you know that there are such horrible pains that you yourself confess, that, upon considering them with a bit of attention, one becomes a fool, and yet, however, you do not become wise. You would become a fool, you say, if you thought of that eternity. You conceive, then, that it is something frightening, but tell me, does not thinking of it make it so that the thing is not or that it would not be for you? If thinking of it has so great an effect, what will it be to suffer it? It is something so frightful, you say, that you cannot think of it, and you do not fear falling into it. This is what I do not understand, and what I will never understand. You do not have the courage to think of death; I am not astonished by this; those more resolved, holier than you, never think of it without trembling. You are horrified to think of eternity, and you fall into it. My God, have pity on us, let Yourself touch our blindness: we do not know what we do, we are poor, senseless men!

Imagine the sorrow and the confusion of a man surprised in a crime, whom human justice casts into a dungeon, among a heap of rascals and evildoers, waiting for his case to be judged. I compare this suffering with that of a Christian who will find himself in hell, in the company of all the hardhearted people there ever were upon earth. In prison, one keeps some hope of escaping, either through flight or through the intrigues and the credit of his friends or through the solicitations and silver of his relatives. One receives some consolation there through the visits of his neighbors and through the cares that they take to provide for your needs, but in hell, who can—or would even want to if he could—console you and risk displeasing God through the compassion he has for your miseries?

The impious, in offending God through their disobedience to the law and through their excesses, seem to me to eat, with the mouth of the body, the precious foods which are served to them, but with the mouth of the heart, they eat iniquity, and what they eat in the world, they will digest in hell, in the midst of eternal torments. Or, if you like it better, the pleasures that they have tasted are like foods which remain in the stomach without being able to be digested, which weigh it down, and which make them pay, with infinite torments, for the moment of sweetness which they caused them in passing through the mouth.

St. Bernard, speaking of the state of the damned, says, "It is certain that the soul is immortal, and that it will not live a single moment without its memory, for fear lest it cease, for a moment, being what it is, in such a way that, while the soul subsists, the memory subsists too. But, O God, what a state! All infected with horrible thoughts through its crimes, puffed up with vanity, hideous through disdain and negligence!

The things which preceded are past and are not; what has been done cannot be undone: thus, although it has been done in time, it will eternally remain having been done; what has passed through time does not pass with time, and consequently, it is an inevitable necessity that you will be eternally tormented by this, that you will eternally remember having done evil."[85]

If it is true that one effectively suffers all the evils that one fears to suffer, what ought one to say of those that one is assured of suffering, as the damned are to suffer them eternally? Pleasures, vain pleasures: who would have told me, when I searched for you with such ardor, when I tasted you with such transport, that your memory would one day be so bitter to me!

---

[85] See St. Bernard, *On Consideration*, V.XII.26 (PL 182:803C–D). La Colombière omits two lines, which fit between these two paragraphs: "Prior things have passed away, and have not passed away. They have passed away from the hand, but not from the mind."

On Hell

It is strange that God was obliged to make a hell in order to stop men from offending Him; after the obligations that we have towards Him, He necessarily believed us very weak or very ungrateful, but it is strange that this same thing does not protect Him from our assaults; God has made hell through zeal for our salvation, but why is it, my God, that You did not give us more knowledge of it, or more fear? Why have You prepared such horrible pains for the sinner, or why have You hidden them from him? He would have plunged himself into all sorts of crimes if You had not stopped his license with this dike; it is true, but he would have avoided even the smallest faults if he had seen the torments with which You punish them. But we were wrong to complain; He did not fail to instruct us, but we do not go over His instructions again, we do not deign to recall them in our memory, we make no effort to penetrate them.

The fire that will surround the body on all sides, into which the damned will be plunged, will burn them without consuming them, in such a way that the skin of each will serve him as a cauldron in which the flesh, the fat, the blood, the marrow in the bones will boil, God giving, adding to the dolorific property—to speak in this way—what He takes away from the consumptive property, giving it the power to insinuate itself, to get mixed up, to enter, to penetrate.[86] This makes you tremble; I tremble, too, at what I am thinking of, and which I don't know how to explain; I tremble when I reflect that all that I conceive is nothing in comparison with what it is. When I will have represented to you, in truth, what the body suffers, what is all that in comparison with what the fire makes the soul to suffer?

Our fire has a thousand uses: it is made for heating, for enlightening, for burning, for cooking, for enjoying, for purifying; that of hell is made only to torment; it is a particular fire, it is called, by the Fathers, an ineffable fire, a marvelous fire, a fire of which one cannot say that it is extinguished, that it is weakened, that it enlightens; this is palpable, liquid, and burning darkness.[87]

---

[86] As Ravier notes, the terms here are from ancient medicine: "dolorific" means "pain-inducing," while "consumptive" means "flesh-consuming" (410, n. 2).

[87] See Lactantius, *Divine Institutes*, VII.XXI: "And yet [the flesh of the damned] will not be that *flesh* which God cast upon man, like the earthly flesh here, but *it will be* insoluble and remaining unto eternity, so that it can suffice for the tortures and the sempiternal fire, whose nature is different from ours here, which we use for the necessities of life, which, unless it is fed with tinder of some kind, is extinguished. But that divine *fire* always lives by itself and thrives without any fuel, nor does it have an admixture of smoke, but it is pure, and liquid, and fluid in the way of water"

If after so many millions of centuries that have passed from the moment when the sun rolled over our heads, the pains of the damned were to cease, I would excuse the disorders of Christians, and I would not take so much trouble to make you quit vice if the pain were not eternal. For a single thought of impurity, a million centuries of flames? Patience! But an eternity? For a thief of an écu, a hell of a hundred million years—O God, what equality!—but finally the pains would cease, and the sight of God—if it could succeed all those tortures and His hate—would efface, in a moment, even the memory of those torments, but faith teaches us that it is for an eternity: and does one find taste in pleasures, and does sin have charms?

(PL 6:801A–B). The notes on the *Divine Institutions* by Joseph Isaeus of Cesena provide many similar references in the Fathers and the Scholastics (PL 6:1011C–1012A). For instance, the Supplement to St. Thomas Aquinas's *Summa Theologiæ* III, q. 97, a. 5–7 discusses many aspects of the fire of hell.

On Paradise

The happiness of the saints, upon considering it through the aspect which is most visible in our regard, consists in this: that they are no longer what we are. We do not know all the goods which they enjoy, but we feel the evils from which they are exempt, and thus, in order to excite ourselves to desire their happiness, it is more advantageous to represent to ourselves the miseries from which they are delivered than the goods which they possess. If the obscure knowledge we have of those ineffable riches does not suffice to make us pant for heaven, the hope of being exempted from so many evils we are overwhelmed by will, doubtless, make us desire paradise. As the surest and most perfect manner of knowing God in this life is to consider the imperfections from which He is exempt, so the shortest and most efficacious way to make us know paradise is to consider the miseries from which it is exempt. The blessed see what we believe, they love what we fear, they possess what we desire.

An infidel is in a state parallel to that of a man who finds himself in the midst of a magnificent parterre[88] during the deepest dark of the night; he hears the sound of the waterfalls and fountains, he smells the scent of the flowers with which it is filled, he can, with his hands, make some judgment of the statues, the trees, and the compartments; when faith enters into this spirit, it is like a torch that one kindles in the middle of the night, which unveils something more, but with that light, all the flowers appear to you as the same color, the greenery has no agreement, the marble is splendorless, half the things escape you, you see it only by pieces, those things which are a bit far off can scarcely be perceived, the symmetry, the relation of the parts, which forms the greatest beauty, escapes you, but when the light of glory is revealed, it is as if the sun appeared all at once; it is at that time that all that appeared to us as dead and languishing becomes, as it were, animated, all laughs, all shimmers, all strikes the eyes, all delights them, all surprises them: one sees, with pleasure, that the ideas which were formed thanks to the torch are infinitely surpassed.

---

[88] A parterre is a type of flower garden with stylized, symmetrical beds and paths; the gardens at the Palace of Versaille are famous examples of parterres.

The saints love what we fear, that is to say, God; their love is no longer mixed with that fear which makes us apprehensive of either losing Him or of having lost Him, lest He punish us eternally for having abandoned Him, or lest He abandon us forever in order to punish our laxness in His service. What pain, to know God, to love Him with all one's heart, and to not know if He loves us or if He hates us, to have only disgust for all the rest, and to doubt if we are agreeable to Him, to languish in expectation of His possession, and to not know if He has resolved to eternally deprive us of His presence! What! To always combat demons, choke passions, vanquish temptations! What! Always in dangers and perils, no moment of surety, everywhere snares and ambushes! What! I fear damning myself, I fear losing my soul and my God, as often as I breathe; one needs only a look, only a thought, to ruin, through reversing, fifty and sixty years of labor and merit; I am divided against myself, I forbid myself all that is most dear to me; all that flatters me could corrupt me, all which is conformed to my nature is an enemy of my virtue, all my senses seek to surprise my reason; I am not even the master of my will, it wants what I do not want, it loves what I hate, it desires what I abhor, it brings me in pursuit of what I flee from: what life, what misery, what torture, what hell!

We will possess, in paradise, what we desire. In the judgment of Saint Thomas, man desires God naturally;[89] this is why the heart always asks for Him under the name of sovereign good. It never deceives itself, this heart, but it is deceived by our understanding, which presents lusts, etc. to it as if they were that good which it pants for; however, it never deceives itself, for it has not embraced this false good; rather, it testifies through its disquiet that this is not what it asks for, that one has ill interpreted its desires; one offers it riches, and one assures it that this is, without a doubt, what it seeks; it believes it, and this belief produces that ardor and that haste that comes to appear in their acquisition. But scarcely has it finally possessed them that it recognizes that it was deceived again,

---

[89] See St. Thomas Aquinas, *Summa Theologiæ* I, q. 60, a. 5: "Therefore, since the universal good is God Himself, and under this good is contained angel and man and every creature, since every creature is naturally, according to what it is, God's; it follows that, by natural love, both angel and man love God more and more principally than themselves. . . .God, inasmuch as He is the universal good, upon which depends every natural good, is loved by each with natural love." See also *ST* I–II, q. 109, a. 3: "To love God above all things is something natural to man, and also to every creature, not only rational, but irrational, and even inanimate, according to the mode of love which can accord with each creature."

and it asks that one seek something else for it, *Inquietum est cor nostrum, donec requiescat in te [Disquieted is our heart until it rests in You]*.[90] It is this which persuades me that, in truth, he seeks God without knowing it, through an instinct which God gave him in creating him. But, as creatures in a crowd, present themselves as as good as God, and as our senses take the creatures for the Creator, they present him that which he does not seek in place of what he seeks. *Num quem desiderat anima mea vidistis [Have you seen whom my soul desires]* (Sg 3:3)? He seems to me like the poor Isaac, blind and enfeebled by his great age: he asks for his elder son, the younger presents himself, his smell and his touch assure him that it is he whom he desires, and he embraces him (Gn 27); or Jacob, who, in truth, has love only for Rachel, and who, however, does not stop from embracing Leah, whom one has substituted in place of her whom he hoped for (Gn 29).

Men who feel that what they desire is a sovereign good and God Himself have made gods of all that they have regarded as their happiness, and they have not doubted that what they believed would satisfy them entirely was above creatures. Thus fathers erected altars

---

[90] St. Augustine, *Confessions*, I.1.1 (PL 32:661).

to their children, husbands to their wives, lovers to their mistresses; those who have regarded gold as the greatest of all goods have adored it as the greatest of all gods, etc.

A cause for joy and for consolation in miseries is to think that in paradise, one will be exempt from them; an illness overwhelms you; say within yourself, "A day will come when my body will be outside the grasp of all the evils which belabor it today, etc., seasons, enemies, passions, temptations, etc."

I do not know what paradise will be; I know that there, one will be plunged into joy, that there, one will see God in Himself, that God does not appear God except in that place of delights, that all the ornaments with which He adorned heaven and earth, all which art could add to nature to cause us pleasure and to charm our senses, all this, I say, is only shadows, nothing in comparison with paradise. But I do not know what will be there. I know what will not be there. No evil—neither moral nor physical—no sin, no vice, no jealousy, no interest, no inconstancy, no power even which could cause pain; more faith, more fear, more hope, more sorrow, no repentance.

You cannot comprehend that one could be happy without the pleasures that you imagine, but tell me, can you comprehend how one could be happy in the exercise of all the most rigorous austerities, when one not only enjoys no bodily pleasure, but when one is in poverty, overwhelmed by maladies, despised, when one fasts, when one tears apart his body by disciplines, when one is consumed by vigils? Yet this is true, and this is so true that there have been saints who made pleasures of all this, who could not live without this. What! The merely obscure knowledge of God, and a bit of love, can sweeten all these sufferings, render them delightful, and clear sight of Him cannot render us happy in a place from which all the evils of this life will be banished, because one will not enjoy certain pleasures there?

Jesus Christ, Who did not deign to accept all the grandeurs, all the delights of earth, although one offered them to Him freely (Mt 4:8–10; Lk 4:5–8), has so esteemed those of heaven that He did not hesitate to suffer death to attain them.

Earth is the exile, or, rather, the gallows, where the saints suffer; heaven is their fatherland and their house of pleasure. Earth, a place of proving, which God has made in such a way that men could not be attached to it.

If He made so terrible a hell for a single mortal sin, human infirmity notwithstanding, He Who is more liberal than He is rigorous, what will He not make for men who have lived a hundred years in the rigors of penitence, despite all the repugnances of nature?

Paradise is the place where God recompenses His servants; there, there must be goods which surpass all those here below; it is where He caresses, where He gratifies, His favorites; one must despair of forming any idea of it.

Our happiness in this life is that we think that we can be what the saints are.

It is easy to imagine the pleasure there is in loving a person who knows our love with ardor, when this passion is not accompanied by jealousy nor by fear, like the saints in paradise.[91]

If the hope of paradise could render the saints happy even amidst the evils of this life, what will the very possession of paradise, without any mixture of evil, do?

None of the evils of this life, none of the goods of this life, no sensible goods, not even any spiritual goods like faith, fear of God, hope; love will remain, but it will become necessary, tranquil.

---

[91] In the first edition, the prior paragraph beginning "A cause for joy and for consolation" is repeated here, with the sole difference of swapping "annoyances" (*ennuis*) for "enemies" (*ennemis*). This repeated paragraph was removed in later editions.

On Paradise

The evils of this life are so great that the pagans themselves, who expected nothing in the other *life*, considered death as a great good.

What has one not done to win paradise? And what sorts of persons, all wise?

There is no moment of calm in this life; one does not know if it is sadness or joy, indigence or riches, pleasure or suffering, which troubles us more; riches and poverty cause almost the same movements of disquieted and deregulated desires. Glory dazes us, confusion overwhelms us, pleasure relaxes our forces and makes us pray for sufferings. In view of this, the pagans considered death as a good.

Glorious immortality, when can we possess you? Ought we to weep or triumph in the memory of your delights and of your grandeurs? Ought we to groan in seeing ourselves as far from you as earth is from heaven? Or ought we rather to rejoice in seeing ourselves as close to you as we are to the end of our exile?

God could make us be born there, bring us there all at once, if He so strongly hoped to make us a part of it. He could, but He willed that we have the pleasure and glory of having merited it. Is it possible that men who suffer such grand labors to have such little goods would run the risk of losing the summit of all goods if one left it to their liberty to acquire it or to neglect it? Is it not enough that one offers it to you—do you want to be forced to receive it? If we envisage heaven every time a creature is presented to tempt us, we would never succumb, but instead of envisaging the world and heaven at the same time, we place the world between us and heaven in order to see naught but the world.

Paradise is the place where God recompenses the saints; it is where He treats them as favored. There is much difference between the conduct of a prince who wants to recompense and that of a king who wants to favor, of a king who wants to make it seen that he is just, and of a king who wants to make it seen that he loves. By merit, one scarcely attains, after much sweat, to a low fortune, to a mediocre fortune, a little higher from one charge to another, but favor does not go so slowly; it is prodigal with goods, it keeps no measure in its liberality, it acts all at once and mixes nothing.